The Minister

A Difference Maker

God Bless You

Robert White

The Minister

A Difference Maker

Robert White

SpiritLife BOOKS

Published in Oxford, Alabama, by SpiritLife Books.

Printed at Pathway Press, Cleveland, Tennessee.

Cover design and photography by Var White.

ISBN: 0-87148-473-0

Printed in the United States of America

Dedications

Kathy White

 This book is dedicated to my loving wife, Kathy, who was reared in a minister's home (Lee and Alma Shires), whose brother (M. A. Shires) was a minister, and who has a call upon her own life. She has been a full partner in ministry with me since we were married at age 21.

 Whenever I accepted a smaller pastorate with smaller pay or moved the family to remote areas of the nation because I believed God was directing us to those assignments, she always went along cheerfully. She has endured hardships, adversity, and, because of limited income, has gone without many things, yet she has never complained.

 A woman of great faith, a true prayer warrior, Kathy is a mighty intercessor who knows how to pray and practices it daily. I have witnessed her faith and prayers moving mountains.

 She is a happy person working for the Lord. I love to hear her sing and hum as she does her work in the home and as we travel in the car to an appointment. Her voice raised in praise creates worship time for us as we travel down America's highways.

Other than commendations from the Lord Him-self and altar results after I have ministered, nothing buoys my spirit like Kathy's smile and her simple words, "You really preached well today." Her smile or pat on the hand lifts me to another plateau; her tears of pain or hurt plunge me into an abyss. She and I have walked hand in hand through many valleys and have stood joyously together on many mountaintops.

Perhaps the greatest tribute I can make to my wife is simply this: When I enter into spiritual warfare, it is Kathy more than any other person I want by my side.

Yes, I dedicate the message of The Minister: A Difference Maker *to her because she has a special understanding of what the ministry is all about. As a minister's daughter, a minister's sister, a minister's wife, and herself a laborer for the Lord, the ministry is all she has ever known. She personifies better than any other person in the world what I am writing about. For this reason, this message is dedicated to my wife, my partner in ministry, my companion, my friend, my encourager. She can by song, by smile, or by prayer help me face every day with confidence knowing it will be a good day.*

Kathy, while you have deserved so much better in life than me, I could never have deserved someone like you.

God is truly an awesome and good God.

Ministers

This book is not dedicated to the masses who masquerade as ministers, but who are in reality wolves in sheep clothing; nor to the hirelings who flee at the first sight of danger; nor to those who are afflicted with the star syndrome; nor to the greedy who make merchandise of the gospel; nor to the abusers who use the message of Christ as a cudgel to club the sheep; nor to those who stand in the pulpit and declare, "Thus saith the Lord" when the Lord has not spoken; nor to those who shut up the kingdom from the hungry seekers; nor to the vain who place themselves above the angels.

Instead, this book is dedicated to the sincere, conscientious multitudes who have had an encounter with God and who will never again be the same; who will preach whether the money is there or not; whose lives are not their own; who approach their responsibilities with fear and trembling lest they miss the Will of God; who weep between the porch and the altar and who pray for souls who refuse to weep or pray for themselves; who reach into the flames and pull sinful men and women from the fire before they slide into a devil's hell; who go about their work largely unappreciated, but who are aware they are bought with a price; whose joy is knowing the power of God, feeling the presence of God, experiencing the anointing of God, and seeing the results of their messages that came not by the will of man but by the Will of God.

This book is dedicated to these very special men and women who know God and who belong to Him. They are the true heroes in this country and in every country where the message of Christ is preached and taught.

They are Ministers. They are Difference Makers.

Contents

Foreword

Life is so precious. It is something to be treasured and cherished, savored and enjoyed. One should start every day thanking the Lord for life and for that day. Whether the sun is shining or the skies are overcast and gray; whether rain or snow, or the earth is bathed in the brilliant rays of the sun, one should realize that it is a beautiful day.

Why is a stormy, cloudy day beautiful? Because you are able to experience it. Life is a gift of God. God created man and breathed the breath of life into his nostrils. Therefore, man is God's creation, made in the image of God and given life that stretches throughout eternity.

Our attitude and spirit reveal how we view life. Instead of taking unimportant things too seriously, we should laugh at all the humorous things that happen to us or around us.

I own my house, but my house doesn't own me. I own my car, not the other way around. All of my possessions are for my benefit and pleasure and are not my masters. Jesus Christ is my Master.

If my wife or son or daughter or three grand-sons make mistakes, how important are those insignificant mistakes? Are they more important than my family's feelings and their sense of self worth?

Also, we should understand the difference between making a name and making a contribution. Charles Dickens made a household name out of Scrooge, one of his fictional characters. Scrooge made a name for himself by being stingy and selfish. Dickens made a contribution; Scrooge made a name for himself, though negative.

Judas and Benedict Arnold made names for themselves for their respective betrayals. Adolph Hitler, Osama bin Laden, and Saddam Hussein are names burned in infamy, but they represent the worst in man's depraved nature.

The bottom line is this: Did a person contribute or destroy? Did that person make the world a better place or a worse place? Are people better off for having known that person?

Is a person a better man or woman because of you, or is that person less of a man or woman? Have you given hope, stirred souls, and challenged people to rise above themselves? Because of you, has someone who was down and out struggled to get up and try one more time? Have you invested time in some young person's life to help him or her avoid some of the pitfalls that befell you in your youth? Have you truly committed to making a mark in life that will bring a smile to the Lord's face? Do you want to repay Christ for His great Gift to you by in turn sacrificing for someone else?

It seems that people who live unto themselves are miserable people. People who never contribute to the good of others rob themselves of some of life's greatest rewards.

It is important that in the brief span of our lives we impact others positively. We should make a contribution, serving God and others; and in this way, leave a legacy of helping others.

How can anybody just live and die without trying to achieve something meaningful?

John Chapman roamed the American wilderness for nearly 50 years planting apple trees. His original name is nearly forgotten, but he is remembered today as Johnny Appleseed. Some trees he planted so long ago even today produce fruit.

Jonas Salk developed a polio vaccine that has saved the lives of countless children.

Benjamin Franklin invented bifocals, the Franklin stove, an odometer, and made advancements in the study of electricity (he also invented the lightning rod).

Inventers, discoverers, scientists, researchers, dreamers, visionaries: each seeks to *achieve something meaningful*.

You may not be in one of these categories, but you can also touch lives, and the lives you touch can touch other lives, and in so doing you can impact heaven and hell. Every person has the power to impact heaven and hell.

Do you truly want your life to count for something, or do you want to live unto yourself?

If you are a baseball player, swing for the fences.

If you are a football player, think touchdown.

If you are a musician, write a song that everyone wants to sing.

If you are a physician, find a cure for diabetes or cancer.

If you are an artist, paint a masterpiece.

If you are an author, write a best seller.

If you are a preacher, preach the anointed Word of God with such passion, fervor, and power that it will melt the hardest and most unbelieving heart, that it will bring revival to the world.

But if you can't hit a homerun? Then hit a single or get on base any way you can.

If you can't score a touchdown? Then block for someone else who can score a touchdown.

If you write a song no one wants to sing? Then write a chorus, or sing your song yourself.

If you don't find a cure, keep searching. And if you don't paint a masterpiece, keep painting. And if you don't write a best seller, keep writing.

And preachers? Keep preaching. No matter what comes; no matter what you see before you; no matter where God takes you. Know that you preach

God's Word, that God's Spirit animates your spirit, and that God will use you for His glory.

Do something that will change the world, change your world, or simply change the world of someone to whom God has directed your life.

Be a difference maker.

Robert White
Oxford, Alabama

Acknowledgments

I am indebted to many people in the preparation and presentation of this book. I appreciate their hard work, suggestions, and confidence that this is a book that honors God and God's ministers, and instructs those same ministers in a way consistent with Holy Scripture.

I am indebted to those who typed, edited, formatted, and prepared the manuscript for publication. I am especially indebted to the following:

- Pastor Ray Dawson, who has himself written an outstanding study on the Minister, provided invaluable input.
- Dr. Alisa R. White helped throughout the creation of this book with insightful suggestions.
- Dr. Joseph E. Jackson gave me wonderful suggestions for strengthening the book.
- Vardaman W. White designed the cover and provided the final edit.

I am indebted most of all to the Holy Spirit, Who dealt with me day and night until I could not rest because of the burning in my heart to tell every minister everywhere, "You are special. You are called of God. You are a difference maker."

Introduction

This message is the product of an assignment I received to prepare a message about the minister. As I prayed and researched the subject both historically and scripturally, the Holy Spirit began to plant the message deep into my spirit.

I sincerely believe that God revealed to me that the minister is the channel through which God will change the world and is changing the world. I am thoroughly convinced that the minister must be a difference maker. He or she cannot, must not settle for business as usual, must not relax in a comfort zone and view the ministry as an employee views his or her job.

We must never think of the ministry as merely a job or occupation. When it becomes a career rather than a calling, when it becomes a way to make money rather than the means to bring people to God, when it becomes what we *do* rather than what we *are*, then we will have lost the ability to make a difference.

No doubt America is facing some of the greatest challenges in her history. The abandonment of moral standards, the breakup of homes, the decline of the traditional family, the abortion tragedy, the open acceptance of sexual immorality, the increasing crime rate, the continued infringement of government upon the rights of individuals, the steady erosion of religious freedom, and many other ills are clear warnings of the dangers that lie ahead for the Church and for the nation.

Where are the difference makers?

The minister is the lone voice in the wilderness denouncing sin and calling a community or city or nation to repentance.

The minister is the warrior leading the charge in tearing down the strongholds of Satan.

The minister is the intercessor chained to an altar of prayer, holding on to the horns of the altar until God is moved on His Throne to bring justice to the abused, neglected, and abandoned spouses and children.

The minister is the shepherd who stands in the gap so that there is no break in the hedge by which the wolf may enter into the sheepfold.

The minister is the stalwart who, when everyone else gives up on a person because of his or her evil deeds, grips that individual firmly and refuses to let go.

The minister is the one who, when the pressures of society make cowards of the brave, and the politicians and elected officials barter away the rights, privileges and freedoms that were secured by our forefathers, steps forward and with a clear voice and strong conviction declares not what is expedient but what "thus saith the Word of the Lord."

The minister is the one who, when betrayed, persecuted, tortured, and facing death can say with

Job, "I know my Redeemer liveth"; can say with Paul, "I have kept the faith" and "I know in whom I have believed"; can say with John Osteen who, on his death bed minutes before leaving this world, propped himself up on one elbow and with the other hand pointed toward heaven and declared, "His mercy endureth forever."

The minister stands between the sinner and a devil's hell. The minister changes the direction of nations and the course of human history. The minister is God's choice, God's anointed man or woman to make a difference.

Yes, God is looking for people who will make a difference. He is looking for people who will "stand in the gap and make up the hedge," who will not settle for the status quo or business as usual.

God does not look for maintainers. He looks for risk takers.

God does not look for comfort seekers. He looks for boat rockers.

God does not look for testers of the wind. He looks for those who will stand for something regardless of personal consequences.

Who are you today? The minister God seeks? The minister God has called?

Let us examine together the minister: who the minister is, what God has called the minister to be and do, and how and why the minister must be a difference maker.

Chapter 1

Difference Makers

I received an email the other day and was deeply moved when I read what happened to the signers of the Constitution of this great nation. The author of the original document is unknown, but I have taken the liberty of listing the facts to make a point.

Men and women had come to America seeking religious freedom and economic benefits. However, British colonialism still oppressed the early settlers. The new world needed men and women who would step forward and provide leadership in throwing off the yoke of colonialism to give birth to a new nation. Yes, a new nation needed difference makers. These men and women would pay a terrible price for the freedom we enjoy today. The sacrifices of the signers of the Constitution were only the beginning.

The British imprisoned Richard Stockton as a traitor for merely signing the Declaration of Independence. Twelve signers' homes were burned. Two had sons who died serving in the Revolutionary Army; another had two sons captured. Seventeen of the signers either fought or rendered medical aid in the Revolutionary War. Many had their property looted or destroyed. A number of them were imprisoned during the War.

The men who signed were educated and wealthy men: lawyers and jurists, farmers and large plantation owners, merchants. Although they had a lot at stake, they signed at great risk, knowing their fates would be uncertain if the British went after them as traitors. By signing, they put everything they had on the line.

Planter and trader Carter Braxton of Virginia lost his ships to the British. He lost more of his holdings in the economic hardships after the war and never recovered.

Thomas McKean was so hounded by the British that he was forced to move his family almost constantly. He served in Congress without pay, and his family was kept in hiding.

Signers George Clymer, William Ellery, Button Gwinnett, Lyman Hall, Thomas Heyward, Arthur Middleton, Edward Rutledge, and George Walton had their property looted by vandals or British soldiers.

According to the ancestors of Thomas Nelson, Jr., British General Cornwallis used the Nelson home for his headquarters. When General George Washington opened fire, the home was destroyed. Nelson died bankrupt.

Francis Lewis' home was destroyed, his wife was jailed, and she died shortly after.

John Hart was driven from his wife's bedside as she was dying. Their 13 children fled for their lives.

When he was able to return home, his wife was dead and his children were gone.

Freedom costs. These men gave up everything: their wealth, their positions, their possessions, and, in many cases, their families and their lives.

They Were Men Of Faith

The historical evidence of their faith is over-whelming. These men and other great leaders of this country proclaimed their strong faith in God and in Jesus Christ.

Every session of Congress begins with a prayer by a paid preacher whose salary has been paid by the taxpayers since 1789. Fifty-two of the 55 founders of the Constitution were members of the established orthodox churches in the colonies.

The first Supreme Court Justice, John Jay, said, "Americans should select and prefer Christians as their rulers."

The voices of these great men might seem faint in light of political expediency today, but there are still men and women of God who refuse to bow a knee to humanism and political correctness.

These brave men were willing to die for their convictions, for a free nation where Christians could serve God without governmental restrictions. They were willing to stand up and be counted. They boldly proclaimed their allegiance to Christ and to pledge the allegiance of the new nation to be a nation "under

God." They wrote upon their currency for the entire world to see, "In God We Trust."

The cap at the top of the Washington Monument in Washington, DC, includes the words "Laus Deo," which is Latin for "Praise be to God." It is one more testimony that America indeed is a nation under God.

Difference makers made it so. We need difference makers to keep it so.

America is a sanctuary for the entire world. Regardless of your faith or your religion, you are welcome to these shores. Our Christian Faith made it so.

In the harbor of New York City stands a beautiful 151-foot lady. Called "Mother of Exiles," our beloved Statue of Liberty says so eloquently,

"Give me your tired, your poor,
Your huddled masses yearning to breathe free,
The wretched refuse of your teeming shore;
Send these, the homeless, tempest-tost to me,
I lift my lamp beside the golden door!"

But there were those welcomed to our shores who betrayed the spirit of that kind lady. While enjoying the privileges of what the Statue of Liberty represents, they sought to rob us of the liberty that our forefathers fought and died to provide.

Slowly but surely, America is today being robbed of her liberties, of her very faith. Even worse, apathy grips the land.

Freedoms Under Attack

When one woman, Madeline O'Hare, attacked prayer in our schools, the Supreme Court, denying the very foundation upon which this nation was built, struck down a practice that was a way of life for most Americans. Next, the Ten Commandments were forbidden to be placed in government buildings. Is this some minor infringement? Absolutely not. Our forefathers stated this was the foundation of all moral and ethical law in this country.

In November, 2003, Chief Justice Roy Moore of the Alabama Supreme Court was removed from office. What was his crime? He refused to obey a federal court order to move a monument of the Ten Commandments from the rotunda of the state courthouse. When Judge Moore was asked why he did not comply with the court order and remove the Ten Commandments, he said, "It would have violated my conscience, violated my oath of office and violated every rule of law I had sworn to uphold" (*Anniston Star*, November 14, 2003).

Judge Moore understands that our entire civil and moral code is based upon the Ten Commandments.

Those who took offense with the presence of the Ten Commandments in the rotunda and who filed the charges against Judge Moore are now trying to get him disbarred. It is not enough for Judge Moore to be removed from office, but his opponents are now determined to limit his influence.

Today, there are efforts to outlaw the pledge of allegiance to the United States of America unless the words after "one nation" – "under God" – are removed.

Defying the moral and spiritual laws set forth by the Judeo-Christian faith as taught in Scripture, some states have approved same-sex relationships. Massachusetts' courts recently struck down a ban on same-sex marriages. Vermont legalized same-sex civil unions. Alaska, California, and the District of Columbia have an official registry for same-sex couples.

Is there an outcry against the raping and plundering of America's religious freedoms? The answer is a resounding "No!"

The nation has been anesthetized. Politicians dare not alienate any radical community of voters. Leaders at every level – city, state, and federal – respond in general terms to convince each community of their support when their only goal is reelection and continuing business as usual.

But in times like these, God always has someone or some group who will stand up.

When Reverend Joe Wright from the Central Christian Church in Wichita was asked to pray before the beginning of the new session of the Kansas House of Representatives in 1996, he prayed: *"Heavenly Father, we come before you to ask your forgiveness.*

We seek your direction and your guidance. We know your word says, 'Woe to those who call evil good.' But that's what we've done.

"We've lost our spiritual equilibrium. We have inverted our values. We have ridiculed the absolute truth of your word in the name of moral pluralism. We have worshiped other gods and called it multiculturalism.

"We have endorsed perversion and called it an alternative lifestyle.

"We've exploited the poor and called it a lottery. We've neglected the needy and called it self-preservation. We have rewarded laziness and called it welfare. In the name of choice, we have killed our unborn. In the name of right to life, we have killed abortionists.

"We have neglected to discipline our children and called it building self-esteem. We have abused power and called it political savvy. We have coveted our neighbor's possessions and called it taxes. We have polluted the air with profanity and pornography and called it freedom of expression. We have ridiculed the time-honored values of our forefathers and called it enlightenment.

"Search us, oh God, and know our hearts today. Try us. Show us any wickedness within us. Cleanse us from every sin and set us free. Guide and bless these men and women who have been sent here

by the people of the State of Kansas, and that they have been ordained by you to govern this great state.

"Grant them your wisdom to rule. May their decisions direct us to the center of your will. And, as we continue our prayer and as we come in out of the fog, give us clear minds to accomplish our goals as we begin this Legislature. For we pray in Jesus' name, Amen."

One Democratic legislator walked out during the prayer in protest. Three others spoke against his prayer, and one labeled the prayer a "message of intolerance."

In 1999, after his daughter, Rachel, was killed and his son, Craig, was wounded in the shootings at Columbine High School in Littleton, Colorado, Darrell Scott was invited to address a House Judiciary Committee's Hearing on Crime. He said, in part:

"I am here today to declare that Columbine was not just a tragedy – it was a spiritual event that should be forcing us to look at where the real blame lies! Much of the blame lies here in this room. Much of the blame lies behind the pointing fingers of the accusers themselves. . . .

"The real villain lies within our own hearts. Political posturing and restrictive legislation are not the answers. The young people of our nation hold the key. There is a spiritual awakening taking place that will not be squelched! We do not need more religion. We do not need more gaudy television evangelists

spewing out verbal religious garbage. We do not need more million-dollar church buildings built while people with basic needs are being ignored. We do *need a change of heart and a humble acknowledgment that this nation was founded on the principle of simple trust in God!"*

Thank God for men who will stand up like Judge Moore, Reverend Wright, and Darrell Scott!

Just as there are attacks on the religious liberties of Americans, so are there attacks on the spiritual liberties of Christianity. The Church needs men and women like those mentioned in Hebrews 11:33-38: "Who through faith subdued kingdoms, worked righteousness, obtained promises, stopped the mouths of lions, quenched the violence of fire, escaped the edge of the sword, out of weakness were made strong, became valiant in battle, turned to flight the armies of the aliens. Women received their dead raised to life again. And others were tortured, not accepting deliverance, that they might obtain a better resurrection. Still others had trial of mockings and scourgings, yes, and of chains and imprisonment. They were stoned, they were sawn in two, were tempted, were slain with the sword. They wandered about in sheepskins and goatskins, being destitute, afflicted, tormented – Of whom the world was not worthy. They wandered in deserts and mountains, in dens and caves of the earth."

If there is truly a champion, a warrior for what is good and right and ethical and godly, few will come from legislatures or courts or from the classrooms of our educational institutions. From where will they come? From the ministry.

I will not take the time here to chronicle the failings of the hirelings and the wolves in sheep's clothing and those who have made merchandise of the gospel. But I will take the time to thank God for a Billy Graham who, whether interviewed on any television program or speaking to a President of the United States, always boldly declared what "thus saith the Lord." His message was simple, but powerful: God loves all sinners, died for us, and salvation comes through Jesus Christ and Christ alone.

Martin Luther King, Jr., abhorring violence, preached civil disobedience against unjust laws and worked to change them. In a powerful speech which was to be his last, he said, "I've been to the mountain-top . . . and I've seen the Promised Land. . . . Mine eyes have seen the Glory of the coming of the Lord." This produces chill bumps on me yet. In another speech, he declared, "I have a dream. . . ." While he did not live to see the fulfillment of the entire dream, his posterity is seeing that dream fulfilled today.

We need men and women of God who have been to the mountaintop, who have a dream and vision of the power of God that will shake a nation, yes, even a world, that will bring about repentance and revival.

Every generation has new challenges and new battles, and so every generation is in need of new champions and new heroes.

God's Signature

Isaiah 43:19: "Behold, I will do a new thing; now it shall spring forth; shall ye not know it?"

It should not surprise anybody that God will do a "new thing" in each situation because that is His signature. He has always done a new thing.

God made Adam from dust. This was new.

God made Eve from Adam's rib. This was new.

God caused the sun to stand still for Joshua. This was new.

Elisha caused an axe head to swim. This was new.

Elisha told Naaman to dip seven times in the river Jordan in order to be healed of leprosy. This was new.

The children of Israel crossed the Red Sea on dry ground. This was new.

God caused an artesian well to start in a rock that produced over 11,000,000 gallons of water per day. This was new.

The children of Israel ate manna baked in the ovens of heaven. This was new.

The children of Israel marched around Jericho for six days and, when they marched seven times on the seventh day, the walls fell flat. This was new.

The Son of God became flesh and was born of a virgin. This was new.

An angelic choir sang at the birth of the Christ child. This was new.

You can only save your life by losing it. This is new.

You can only save what you give away. This is new.

We need ministers who are in tune with God, anointed by God, and who are led by His Spirit. We must never forsake the "old paths" having to do with theology and the doctrines of Christ, but we must be sensitive to the Holy Spirit as God leads us to new methods to reap the greater harvest.

In times like these, who can step up and be counted? From what segment of society and from which community will difference makers emerge?

The ministry.

Why? The minister is called to special services. While all Christians serve, others choose a profession, work for wages, work for man.

The minister is called. Called of God. Called to represent God. Called to obey God. Called to declare the words of God given to him or her by God.

God's Call

There are not many people today in American politics or in the commercial world who will risk all to stand up for Jesus Christ or for the moral and civil laws based upon Scripture. Few will sacrifice all they have to protect the freedom of religion and other liberties enjoyed by this nation. Even some ministers will compromise because the call to the world is to them stronger than the call by God.

There are three calls I will mention here. The first two I will present very briefly because the focus of this book is about the third call.

The Call to Repentance

There is a universal call from God to every sinner to repent and be saved. It is not His will that any should perish, but that all come to repentance.

2 Peter 3:9: "The Lord is not slack concerning His promise, as some count slackness, but is long-suffering toward us, not willing that any should perish but that all should come to repentance."

God does not want anyone to perish but wants all – *a-l-l* – to come to repentance. If you go to hell, you will have to trample His blood beneath your feet. You will have to reject every provision He has made for you.

This call is reflected in the very theme of the New Testament stated in John 3:16: "For God so loved the world that He gave His only begotten son that whoever believes on Him should not perish but have everlasting life."

Redemptive grace goes beyond the house of David to the entire world:

"For the grace of God that brings salvation has appeared to all men" (Titus 2:11).

"And it shall come to pass, that whoever shall call on the name of the Lord shall be saved" (Acts 2:21).

"Whoever confesses that Jesus is the Son of God, God abides in him, and he in God" (1 John 4:15).

"Whoever believes in Him shall not perish but have eternal life" (John 3:15).

"Whoever lives and believes in Me shall never die" (John 11:26).

The word *whoever* or *whosoever* is an all-inclusive pronoun. It includes every human being on earth regardless of language or culture, whether tall or short, educated or uneducated, rich or poor.

The word *whosoever* was written in blood on the Cross of Calvary.

The word *whosoever* was written on the gates of hell by resurrection power.

The word *whosoever* was written on the empty tomb by a Risen Savior.

The word *whosoever* was written in the Upper Room by the Rushing Mighty Wind.

And the word *whosoever* means you today if you are a sinner.

The Call to Service

If you are born again, God is calling you to service. The believer is to totally and wholly follow the Lord. Every believer is to be a minister. Every believer is a worker.

When a demon-possessed man was delivered by Christ and then desired to go with the Lord, the Word said, "Jesus did not permit him, but said to him, 'Go home to your friends, and tell them what great things the Lord has done for you, and how He has had compassion on you'" (Mark 5:19). Jesus did not call the demonic to one of the fivefold ministries, but sent him home to witness about the "great things the Lord has done for" him.

We are to be workers in His vineyard. We are to praise and worship. We are to pray and intercede.

Jesus said the harvest is great but the laborers are few. In other words, there are too many bench-warmers. If you can drive, accept the call to drive the church bus. If you are a mechanic, accept the call to keep the lawn mower and church bus repaired. If you have a way with children, accept the call to work in the nursery. If you are a prayer, accept the call to work with the intercessors. If you are successful in business, accept the call to be a pastor's helper and minister to him or her. Be like Aaron and Hur holding up the hands of the anointed one. Accept the call to be an armor-bearer to protect the back of the pastor.

Each one of us is to be a sender. We are to support the various ministries and, in particular, the ministers themselves.

When Israel possessed Canaan, every tribe was given a parcel of land as an inheritance, except for the tribe of Levi. Why? Because the tribe of Levi was composed of the priests or ministers.

God has a great plan. The congregation neither hires nor pays the minister. Instead, the congregation gives God the tenth that belongs to Him, plus their offerings. Out of what they give to God, God then pays the minister. Simple, isn't it?

The believers or congregation also "ordain" ministers. Ordination is a biblical term indicating that a congregation or organization recognizes God's ordination of someone into the ministry. The congregation then officially ordains that person as an act of approval.

In Acts 13:2, the Word tells us that the Holy Spirit said, "Now separate to Me Barnabas and Saul for the work to which I have called them." In verse 3, we read, "they laid hands on them and sent them away."

In 1 Timothy 4:14, Paul tells Timothy not to neglect the gift given him by prophecy with the laying on of hands. And in 1 Timothy 2:7, Paul states that he was ordained a preacher and an apostle.

I encourage you to study 1 Corinthians 12 regarding the various gifts, the distribution of those gifts, and how each relates to the other.

In the next chapter, I will discuss in greater detail the call to ministry. I will then turn attention to the nature of this ministry and to those whom God has called.

Chapter 2

The Call to Minister

Ephesians 4:11-12: "And He Himself gave some to be apostles, some prophets, some evangelists, and some pastors and teachers, for the equipping of the saints for the work of ministry, for the edifying of the body of Christ. . . ."

We find the entire fivefold ministry contained in this one verse of Scripture. This broad subject warrants an entire book dedicated to just this one study; therefore, I will not attempt to deal with it here except to acknowledge these various ministries.

I will share with you briefly a conversation I had with Rich Bowen, pastor of the great New Hope Worship Center in Augusta, Georgia. He stated that a simple way to keep the fivefold ministries in focus is to look at your hand.

The thumb represents the ministry of the Apostle. The thumb controls the function of the hand. Therefore, the concise definition of the Apostle would be *one who governs*.

The index finger represents ministry of the Prophet. The index finger is the pointing finger on the hand. Therefore, the definition of the Prophet would be *one who guides*.

The ministry of the Evangelist is the middle finger, which is the longest finger on the hand. The definition of the Evangelist is the *one who gathers*. He is the soul winner.

The finger between the middle finger and the little finger represents the Pastor. The Pastor is the *one who guards and protects*.

The ministry of the Teacher is the fifth finger. The Teacher is the *one who grounds and establishes*.

I will not elaborate on this illustration since the fivefold ministries are not the focus of this book. Still, they serve as a good representation of the roles of the minister.

I want to look specifically at the minister as a difference maker. There is laid upon the minister the privilege of obligation and sacrifice. The Good News without the good deed will leave you impotent and powerless. The title of "minister" without the scriptural function will lead you to disillusionment.

There was a time when the minister was the most respected person in a community. In the early days of our country, the first building that was built in a new settlement was the church. Why? Because it was central to the activities and life of the township.

Look at the situation today: Years of ministers betraying the trust of their congregations and their communities have eroded the confidence of the public. Some high-profile ministers in America have confessed their sins. One of the most influential and powerful denominations in America is rocked with scandal because of the conduct by some of its priests. A leading denomination recently elected as Bishop a man living openly in an "alternative lifestyle." These actions by priests and clergy have fostered a sense of betrayal among their publics.

Yet one could make a case from the Bible that this is an age-old problem. Lucifer, one of the arch-angels, rebelled against God. One out of every three angels joined in Lucifer's rebellion. Even one of the Twelve who lived with Christ and witnessed His life, His teachings, and His miracles betrayed Him for 30 pieces of silver. I could fill a book just chronicling the misdeeds of the clergy.

So why this message? Because God-called and God-anointed men and women are still the most important persons in any community. And many are doing their best to represent Christ faithfully.

When Elijah sat under the juniper tree and com-plained that he was the only one doing right, God reprimanded him by saying He had 7,000 who had never bowed a knee to Baal. May I remind you that while Lucifer is still in rebellion, Gabriel, another archangel, is still carrying messages of God throughout the universe? Michael, another archangel, is still fighting your battles. While one third of the angels followed Lucifer, two thirds of the angels withstood him. They also encamp around those who fear the Lord. While Judas betrayed the Lord, 10 of the remaining 11 disciples gave their lives in a martyr's death, singing the praises of victory. While you can find sin in high as well as humble places in the church, multitudes of ministers sacrifice every day and go about their God-given responsibilities without complaint and without recognition.

2 Timothy 4:3: "For the time will come when they will not endure sound doctrine, but according to their own desires, because they have itching ears, they will heap up for themselves teachers; and they will turn their ears away from the truth, and be turned aside to fables." Then, verse 5: "But you be watchful in all things, endure afflictions, do the work of an evangelist, fulfill your ministry."

When you preach, are you an entertainer or a herald of Jesus Christ? Are you a performer or a messenger sent from the glory world to pull sinners out of hell?

Jesus was taken to an exceeding high mountain where the devil showed Him all the kingdoms of the world. He told Jesus that he would give them to Jesus if Jesus would bow down and worship him. At some time in your ministry, the devil is going to take you to that high mountain and show you what he can do for you. He will offer you money or prestige or power to do his bidding. He will seek to discover your price. He will offer you shortcuts to success. "Jesus, you don't have to suffer and die to get these kingdoms." The devil will tell you that you don't have to fast and pray and sacrifice to be successful. He doesn't care if you preach to crowds or if you are rich and affluent and are popular as long as you don't preach the whole truth.

When confronted by Satan, remember one thing. It is easier to stand for truth and right, knowing that God will see you through, than it is to get back what you have sold to the devil.

When asked to change his policies on emancipation, President Abraham Lincoln said, "I am a slow walker, but I never walk backwards." As ministers, we may take the slow and steady approach, but we must always move forward, never backward. Our backs must always be to temptation and the devil's snares.

William Morley Punshon, a nineteenth century English Wesleyan minister, said, "Cowardice asks, Is it safe? Expediency asks, Is it politic? Vanity asks, Is it popular? But conscience asks, Is it right?" The minister must ask the same question in any situation: "Is it right?" Then, the minister's actions must conform to the answer to that question: *do what is right.*

Matthew 11:7-9: "As they departed, Jesus began to say to the multitudes concerning John: 'What did you go out into the wilderness to see? A reed shaken by the wind? But what did you go out to see? A man clothed in soft garments? Indeed those who wear soft clothing are in kings' houses. But what did you go out to see? A prophet? Yes, I say to you, and more than a prophet.'"

Jesus asked the question, "What did you go out to see?" When people attend your church or go to hear you preach, what do they expect to see and what do they really see and hear? If they know you to be a man or woman of honor, a man or woman who does what is right, a man or woman who lives the life about which you preach, then expectations and reality will be the same: they will expect the truth, and they will hear the truth. But if you have undermined your reputation by turning the focus of your services away from God and toward yourself, by doing what is expedient rather than what is right, by – in short – falling to temptation, then everything they hear is also undermined, tainted, by their perception of you.

As a minister, you lose your effectiveness.

To be effective, the minister must understand the answer to three questions:

Who called you?

What did He call you to be?

What did He call you to do?

In the next few chapters, we will address these vital questions.

Chapter 3

Who Called You?

The ministry is the greatest calling and work in the world. You represent Someone greater than any country or corporation or business. You represent the God of Glory. You didn't choose Him; He chose you.

As a young man, when I interviewed for a job, I told them everything good and positive – and nothing bad or negative – about myself. But when God came calling, I told Him everything bad about myself and nothing positive. God already knew all about me and He wanted me anyway.

Galatians 1:15-16: "But when it pleased God, who separated me from my mother's womb and called me through His grace, to reveal His Son in me, that I might preach Him among the Gentiles. . . ."

2 Timothy 1:8-9: "Therefore do not be ashamed of the testimony of our Lord, nor of me His prisoner, but share with me in the sufferings for the gospel according to the power of God, who has saved us and called us with a holy calling, not according to our works, but according to His own purpose and grace which was given to us in Christ Jesus before time began."

1 Corinthians 1:26-29: "For you see your calling brethren, that not many wise according to the flesh, not many mighty, not many noble, are called. But God has chosen the foolish things of the world to put to shame the wise, and God has chosen the weak things of the flesh to put to shame the things which are mighty; and the base things of the world and the things which are despised God has chosen, and the things which are not, to bring to

nothing the things that are, that no flesh should glory in His presence."

We were nothing when God called us, yet we can defeat the most wise and powerful of this world through Christ.

2 Corinthians 4:7: "But we have this treasure in earthen vessels, that the excellence of the power may be of God and not of us."

1 Timothy 1:12-13: "And I thank Christ Jesus our Lord who has enabled me, because He counted me faithful, putting me into the ministry, although I was formerly a blasphemer, a persecutor, and an insolent man; but I obtained mercy because I did it ignorantly in unbelief."

A Divine Purpose

Acts 26:16: "But rise and stand on your feet, for I have appeared to you for this purpose, to make you a minister and a witness both of the things which you have seen and of the things which I will yet reveal to you."

Those men and women called of God have a purpose in life: a divine purpose.

From these Scriptures we learn that God calls us, makes us, and puts us in the ministry through a sovereign act. This treasure, which is Jesus Christ, is in an earthen vessel; in this way, no flesh should receive the glory. The value of the vessel depends upon what is inside. It is all about Jesus.

He called us and He is our source. We are accountable to Him. He will judge what is success or failure.

If you are pastoring in some remote area to which God called you, then you are as faithful as the pastor of the largest church in America, and in the eyes of God you are just as successful. It doesn't matter what people think. God's standard for success is different than the world's standard of success. Never embrace the world's value system.

My purpose in life is to preach. That is my life's work, my life's purpose, my life's calling.

What separates the ministry from all other professions and careers? What causes the minister to weep when the body is worn out, when old age has drained him or her of energy and has blunted physical and intellectual skills to where the minister can no longer fill a pulpit?

The calling.

The call of God.

The President of the United States, after serving his term of office, leaves politics and becomes a statesman. He has achieved the highest political office in the land and there are no more worlds to conquer.

But not the minister.

The athlete, after breaking the home run record in baseball, or the sack record or touchdown record in football, may retire and reap the rewards of those accomplishments.

But not the minister.

The author or artist may retire after writing the best seller or painting the masterpiece.

But not the minister.

The inventor and businessperson may accomplish great things, may become a part of history through those great feats, and may retire to rest upon their laurels.

But not the minister.

Like Beethoven's unfinished symphony, the minister's work – regardless of how impressive or seemingly successful – is never finished.

The minister isn't a nine-to-five employee.

The minister isn't a forty-hour per week worker.

The minister isn't a five days per week worker.

The minister isn't unionized.

The minister doesn't lobby for shorter hours.

The minister doesn't have enough hours in the day nor days in the week to do the needed job. But the minister understands that the work is not a job.

The minister is on a mission. Because of the call, his or her work is only finished when God calls the minister home. The minister is a minister until death.

There is a difference in a career and a calling.

Lot had a career; Abraham had a calling.

Cain had a career; Abel had a calling.

Ishmael had a career; Isaac had a calling.

Esau had a career; Jacob had a calling.

The ten spies had a career; Joshua and Caleb had a calling.

Simon the sorcerer had a career; Simon Peter had a calling.

Pharaoh had a career; Moses had a calling.

Potiphar had a career; Joseph had a calling.

Haman had a career; Esther had a calling.

Ahab had a career; Elijah had a calling.

Nebuchadnezzar had a career; Shadrach, Meshach, and Abednego had a calling.

Darius had a career; Daniel had a calling.

Goliath, the giant, had a career; little David had a calling.

King Saul had a career; King David had a calling.

Herod had a career; John the Baptist had a calling.

King Agrippa had a career; the Apostle Paul had a calling.

Pilate had a career; Jesus had a calling.

You must have a relationship with God that transcends all other relationships. My greatest earthly relationship is with my wife. She is my wife, companion, sweetheart, partner, counselor, prayer and ministry partner, encourager; she is everything a wife could be to a husband in ministry. But there is one relationship that transcends wife, son, daughter, or anyone or anything else: my relationship with God. If my relationship with God becomes flawed, then my life is flawed and must be repaired.

If you are not sold out to God whereby your ministry is a consuming fire, an addiction that impacts every fiber of your being, then you need another visit to Calvary. My relationship with God is a life and death matter.

You cannot defeat a man or woman who has God's call. The call drives a minister on while the hireling falls by the wayside.

The call keeps the shepherd by the sheep when the hireling flees.

The call keeps the missionary walking for days to minister to some remote village when the hireling will only travel first class to an appointment.

The call drives the minister to the street corner, nursing home, or jail to preach or witness while the hireling will only preach in the largest churches when guaranteed a large offering.

The call keeps the minister on his or her knees – sometimes all through the night – while the hireling cannot pray for a single hour.

The call keeps the minister on bended knees weeping for the souls of lost men and women while the eyes of the hireling remain dry.

Why? Because the call is from God. There is no replacement for that call. A call by any other than God is not the same, does not have the same urgency, does not have the same power, does not have the same authority, and does not have the same claim upon our lives.

Who called you if you are truly a minister? I did not; nor did your mother or father, your aunts or uncles, your grandparents or grandchildren, your pastor or missionary. If you are called, the call is God's call. God's call is the only call worth answering, the only call worth dying for, the only call worth living for.

We know now from whence comes the call. But what has God called us to? Let us address these in the next chapters.

Chapter 4

What Has God Called You to Be?

You cannot represent God if you do not have a relationship with Him, and in this relationship you are changed into a new creature. What you *are* is more important than position or title. What you *do* flows from what you *are*.

First and foremost, you must be a man or woman of God. If your relationship with God becomes flawed, then your life is flawed and must be repaired. If you are not sold out to God so that your ministry is a consuming fire, an addiction that impacts every fiber of your being, then you need another visit to Calvary. It bears repeating: your relationship with Christ is a life and death matter.

Psalms 104:3-4: "He lays the beams of His upper chambers in the waters, Who makes the clouds His chariot, Who walks on the wings of the wind, Who makes His angels spirits, His ministers a flame of fire."

The minister as a flame of fire is to touch the dry stubble of dead churches and bring revival fires to them.

My questions to you are these:

What kind of minister do you want to be?

What is your goal or objective in life?

What do you think God has specifically called you to do?

What do you think your main responsibilities are as a minister?

If God asked you the one thing you want Him to do for you, what would it be?

How do you want to be remembered?

When the devil takes you to the top of a mountain and shows you the kingdoms of the world – the fame or fortune or power he can give you – how will you respond?

When your world is turned upside down, when you are walking through the valley, how will you respond?

When your character and integrity are challenged and nobody will know whether you sell out or not, what will your answer be?

What you are as a minister determines the answers to these questions.

Paul said in Acts 20:24: "But none of these things move me; nor do I count my life dear to myself, so that I may finish my race with joy, and the ministry which I received from the Lord Jesus, to testify to the gospel of the grace of God." Then, in verses 26-27: "Therefore I testify to you this day that I am innocent of the blood of all men. For I have not shunned to declare to you the whole counsel of God."

What greater testimony can anyone have than to be able to say I have declared the whole counsel of God? I not only preached heaven, but I preached hell. I preached the blessings of the Lord, but also the judgment of the Lord. I preached it all.

But how do we preach the judgment and preach hell? Do we preach from our own judgmental, harsh, legalistic perspective? Or do we preach it with tears and weeping?

Jeremiah 9:1: "Oh that my head were waters and my eyes a fountain of tears that I may weep day and night for the slain of the daughter of my people!"

The man and woman of God aren't as concerned about being "politically correct" as they are about doing what "thus saith the Lord."

I would rather go to a church with only one member and have God go with me than to go to the largest church in the denomination and go there without Him.

God's standards are different from the world's standards and His value system is different from the world's value system. The world derives its power from money and numbers, but the Word says, "not by might nor by power but by My Spirit says the Lord of Hosts" (Zechariah 4:6). The world says to retaliate and exact vengeance; Christ said to turn the other cheek. If a man forces you to go one mile, then go two miles. If a man takes your coat, then give him your cloak, also.

The world wants you to tickle their ears and entertain them, but John the Baptist stood at Herod's gate and cried, "It isn't lawful for you to have your brother's wife."

The world wants you to give a performance, but Christ would have you preach the Word with Holy Ghost power to convict the sinner of sins and to bring healing, miracles, and deliverance to the captives.

The world would have you wear the medals of honor or dishonor, but Paul said, "I bear in my body the marks of the Lord Jesus." Show me your medals and I will show you my scars.

I am not as concerned with how many attend a service as I am with what happens to those who attend the service. What is important is not what happens in your campmeeting or conference, but what happens at the judgment of rewards when Christ says "Well done."

Man cannot determine my height or the number of hairs on my head.

Man cannot determine absolutely my health or the number of my days.

Man cannot raise me from the dead, nor give me a new body.

Man cannot guarantee my condition in the hereafter.

Man cannot provide for me a mansion in heaven, nor give me fruit from the Tree of Life, nor water from the River of Life.

But God can.

God is my Source, my Commander-in-Chief, my Savior, my Provider, My Protector, My Comforter, and my Deliverer.

To Be a Servant

Leadership Ministries Worldwide published a book, *What the Bible Says To The Minister*, in which "minister" is defined: "The word 'minister' means an under-rower. It refers to the slaves who sat in the belly of the large ships and pulled at the great oars to carry the boat through the sea. Christ is the Master of the ship and the minister is one of the slaves of Christ. Note: you are only one of many under-rowing servants. Remember also that slaves in the belly of the ship were bound by chains. They were allowed to do nothing but serve the master of the ship. You are a bond slave of Christ: you exist only to row for the Master. You do not and cannot serve anyone else."[*]

---

[*] Used by permission. Leadership Ministries Worldwide, Chattanooga, Tennessee.

In Martin Luther King's sermon, "The Drum Major Instinct," he preached that Christ redefined what it means to be great: the greatest are our servants. From this, Dr. King rejoices that being great is now available to all of us because all of us have the ability to serve.

The very definition of "minister" is that of "servant." Serving is not simply what the minister does, but it is part of the minister's very nature.

What the Bible Says To The Minister also addresses the triumph of the minister as well as his work: "God always causes you to triumph. As a true minister of God, you will never know defeat – not permanently. Even if you fall and fail for a period of time, God will eventually reach you and restore you and He will continue to use you. God will always cause His dear minister to triumph over all. There is nothing, absolutely nothing, that can conquer and gain the final victory and triumph over you – not if you are truly called of God – not if you truly serve Him. The glorious triumph over all is assured."

Romans 8:35-39: "Who shall separate us from the love of Christ? Shall tribulation, or distress, or persecution, or famine, or nakedness, or peril, or sword? As it is written, for Your sake we are killed all day long; we are accounted as sheep for the slaughter. Yet in all these things we are more than conquerors through him that loved us. For I am persuaded that neither death nor life, nor angels nor principalities nor powers, nor things present nor things to come, nor height nor depth, nor any other created thing, shall be able to separate us from the love of God, which is in Christ Jesus our Lord."

Yes we are love slaves, servants of the Most High God, but we are also conquerors through Him Who loved us and gave Himself for us.

It is the minister's nature to serve. It is the minister's destiny to conquer.

To Be a Watchman

Isaiah 21:11: ". . . Watchman, what of the night? Watchman, what of the night?"

Ezekiel 3:17-19: "Son of man, I have made you a watchman for the house of Israel; therefore hear the word at My mouth, and give them warning from me: When I say unto the wicked, You shall surely die; and you give him no warning, nor speak to warn the wicked from his wicked way, to save his life, that same wicked man shall die in his iniquity; but his blood will I require at your hand. Yet, if you warn the wicked, and he does not turn from his wickedness, nor from his wicked way, he shall die in his iniquity; but you have delivered your soul."

Isaiah 56:10-11: "His watchmen are blind; they are all ignorant, they are all dumb dogs, they cannot bark; sleeping, lying down, loving to slumber. Yes, they are greedy dogs which never have enough, and they are shepherds who cannot understand; they all look to their own way, every one for his own gain, from his own territory."

While the enemy is storming the gates to the city, you can hear today's watchman calling out, "All is well. All is well." The true watchman, though, speaks the truth whether it is popular or not, whether it is what people want to hear or not. A true watchman understands his or her role: to stay awake, to be vigilant, to keep watch lest attacks come. We need true watchmen who watch for the souls of mankind and who cry out a warning when the enemy approaches.

To Be Compassionate

Matthew 9:36: "But when he saw the multitudes, He was moved with compassion for them, because they were weary and scattered, like sheep having no shepherd."

One thing that bothers me about the famous ministers I referred to in my introduction is that many have dynamic personalities, high IQs, and good researchers who prepare good material for them; but I never see them weep. Too many preachers can quote chapter after chapter of Scripture and page after page of Encyclopedias, but they have no tears. Theirs is a performance. Theirs is merely a production.

When have you prayed all night for souls? When have you had such a burden that it seemed as if an elephant were standing on your chest crushing out your very life? You could barely breathe, yet you prayed. God give us compassion for hurting people and lost souls!

I confess to you I am not a great prayer. I don't pray as I should, so please do not misunderstand me when I tell you that in the last two or three years, Kathy and I have prayed all night several times. Why? Because I must go to the Rock when I am overwhelmed. The Rock is higher, taller, stronger than I am. I must plant my feet *there* to be the minister God called me to be.

God didn't call us to scatter the sheep or wound the sheep. No, God called us to gather and feed the sheep. But how many ministers do not weep for the sheep, do not care whether they are in the sheepfold and are well fed?

God didn't call us to ignore the masses and to cater only to the wealthy. But how many ministers are more interested in cultivating relationships with the well-to-do than in getting dirty ministering to the needs of the poor and desolate?

To Be Forgiving

The fact that ministers are compassionate is related to the fact that we are also forgivers.

Luke records the words of Jesus on the Cross:

Luke 23:34: "Then Jesus said, 'Father forgive them for they do not know what they do.' And they divided His garments and cast lots."

The Book of Acts records the words of Stephen:

Acts 7:60: "Then he knelt down and cried out with a loud voice, 'Lord do not charge them with this sin.' And when he had said this he fell asleep."

Stoned by an angry mob, as Stephen lay dying he prayed for forgiveness for those who stoned him just as Jesus prayed for forgiveness for His crucifiers.

You might say, "This is really tough." You would be right: It *is* tough. Who you are as a minister, as one of great compassion, is not dependent on how you are treated. Frankly, there will be many times when you as a minister will be mistreated. But how you respond will determine your own victory and success. You respond with the forgiveness of Christ. Why? Because you *embody the forgiveness of Christ as His minister!*

I remember very vividly the funeral of June Williams, the wife of a very dear friend and successful pastor in Alabama, and the mother of another successful pastor. A perfect family, and all serving God in the ministry. In

March 2003, a man just released from prison robbed the funeral home that Sister Williams directed; he killed three people, execution style, including June Williams. At the funeral, I listened to one of the greatest funeral messages I have ever heard given by the victim's son, Terry Williams. As I listened, I marveled, especially as he said, "I would give anything if I could hug my mother one more time, but I can't. But I forgive the man who murdered her. I pray for him that he will be saved and will escape hell."

I marveled because I sat there dealing with my own anger. My feelings were for the murderer to go on to his swift and harsh reward. But this son, hurting far more than I was, told the mourners that he had forgiven. He, in fact, was praying for the murderer.

When Edwin Williams, June's husband, stood up, I wondered what he would say. What would be his attitude? He told the congregation that when he first went to the funeral home and saw his wife, he started crying. All night he cried; all the next day he cried; all the next night he cried. But, then, the Holy Spirit touched him and gave him peace. The night before the funeral, comforted, he slept.

Reverend Williams said, "I have preached it many times, but I can say to all that are present that it is true. God will never leave you nor forsake you, but will go with you all the way. In your darkest hour, He will be there."

I confess that I have never gone through anything as devastating as this wonderful family. Their words, the attitudes they showed, the love and compassion, the comfort and peace, touched my heart. Yes, even when your heart is breaking you can still forgive and experience victory through Jesus Christ! No matter your circumstances, you can still know the joy of the Lord!

I once heard the testimony of Cindi Lamb, who co-founded Mothers Against Drunk Drivers (MADD) after her daughter had been run over and killed by a drunken driver. She went to Howard Hancock's church in Baltimore and received Christ into her heart. On the day she was baptized, she visited the man who ran over her child and told him she forgave him.

Minister, if you have anything in your heart against a church or a church official, a minister or member, get it under the Blood of Jesus. You must forgive if you are ever to experience the joy of the Lord again.

Another testimony, this time of a man and a younger man, perfectly illustrates what I am saying. In a television appearance, the gentleman related that he had stood in the driveway of his home, had hugged his wife and little girl, then had watched them drive down the street. Soon after, a young man who was drag racing hit the car and killed both beloved wife and daughter. We can only imagine the grief of this husband and father. What he must have gone through for the next few months!

Eventually, the man visited the young man in prison. In that prison, the young man asked the man whom he had so terribly wronged to forgive him. He told him how truly sorry he was for what he had done.

The older man looked at this prisoner and saw his grief and repentant spirit. He told the young man that he forgave him.

After that first visit, he saw the young man several times. Now, the two of them speak at high schools, share their testimonies, and tell about the dangers of drag racing.

When the man was asked how he could forgive the killer of his wife and daughter, he replied that only when he forgave him did he get his own life back.

May I ask? Do *you* have *your* life back? Have you never forgiven some wrong done to you? Have you dwelled on this wrong, allowing it to sap you of your spiritual vitality? Remember the words of Christ in Mark 11:26: "But if you do not forgive, neither will your Father which is in heaven forgive your trespasses." It is impossible to receive forgiveness unless we ourselves forgive.

God's wonderful grace is sufficient if we will trust Him. He appropriates His grace to us only when we need it. Standing on the sidelines, situations arise in other people's lives that cause us to marvel at their forgiveness and attitude. But when those situations arise in our own lives, we discover the measure of grace we need for that particular situation.

To Be Prepared

Pastor Ray Dawson, in a Bible lecture, told the story of a minister who was preparing to preach one Sunday morning in a prison chapel service. He visited the prison on Saturday to receive an orientation. The warden escorted him to the 1,500-seat chapel auditorium where he noticed two chairs covered in black. In reply to his question, the warden told him that the two men who would sit in those chairs on Sunday would be executed on Monday. The sermon they would hear on Sunday would be the last sermon they would ever hear.

Shaken, the minister left the prison. Later, as he began to study his sermon, he tore it up. He realized that it was not sufficient for the two men who would be hearing a sermon for the last time.

The question for all ministers is this: Do you realize that every time you preach, you may be preaching the last sermon someone will ever hear?

Jeremiah 23:4: "I will set up shepherds over them who will feed them and they shall fear no more, nor be dismayed, nor shall they be lacking says the Lord."

Jeremiah 3:15: "And I will give you shepherds (pastors) according to My heart who will feed you with knowledge and understanding."

God is looking for shepherds, men and women who will feed the flock of God, who will protect and heal and nurture the flock.

John 10:12: "But a hireling, he who is not the shepherd, one who does not own the sheep, sees the wolf coming and leaves the sheep and flees; and the wolf catches the sheep and scatters them."

John 10:15: "As the Father knows Me, even so I know the Father and I lay down My life for the sheep."

The shepherd cannot tend to the flock without proper preparation. The staff, knowledge of the sheep, understanding of the wiles of the wolf, and more are required. So, too, the minister must be prepared, understanding God's Word and those charged to his or her care.

To Be Anointed

". . . the LORD has anointed me. . ." (Isaiah 61.1).

You can do many things without the anointing: you can depend upon your memory, your charismatic personality, or your education, but you cannot impact heaven and hell without His anointing. You can build buildings and obtain positions of power and influence, but you cannot say to the lame and crippled, "Silver and gold I do not have, but what I do have I give you: In the name of Jesus Christ of Nazareth, rise up and walk" (Acts 3:6). You cannot confront the demons of hell in the name of Jesus Christ. Yes, you can impact the work without God's anointing, but you cannot impact heaven without His anointing.

Mark 16:17-18: "And these signs will follow those who believe: In My name they will cast out demons; they will speak with new tongues; they will take up serpents; and if they drink anything deadly, it will by no means hurt them; they will lay hands on the sick, and they will recover."

You cannot have His anointing without spending time in His presence. When the disciples asked Jesus why they failed to heal the sick, Jesus said, "This comes by prayer and fasting" (Mark 9:29).

Minister, this is a powerful story in Mark 9. A father brought his son, who was afflicted by a deaf and dumb spirit. The disciples tried to cast out the evil spirit, but failed. The father took the child to Jesus. Hear his plea: "have compassion on us and help us" (Mark 9:22).

This distraught father had witnessed his boy being thrown into the fire by this spirit. He had anguished and hurt with his son for years. Now he asked Jesus to have compassion, not just on the boy, but also on *us*.

When a member of a family is suffering, the entire family suffers. When one hurts, the entire family hurts. When you minister to one, you minister to the entire family. When you deliver one, you deliver the entire family.

The disciples asked Jesus, "Why could we not cast him out?" Jesus replied, "This kind can come forth by nothing, but by prayer and fasting."

Yes, you can entertain, you can perform, you can organize and administer without this power. But if you want to have power over demons and devils, you must have an anointing that only comes by fasting and praying, that is only possible by getting very close to God.

1 Timothy 2:1: "Therefore I exhort first of all that supplications, prayers, intercessions, and giving of thanks be made for all men." Paul emphasized that his instructions regarding prayer should be primary among his instructions ("first of all").

Four kinds of prayer are mentioned in this verse. The first is supplication, which generally consists of making our petitions known. We supplicate in prayer for forgiveness, for blessings, for material provision and for numerous other things that come as favors. In his *Exposition of the Whole Bible*, John Gill wrote that this first type of prayer "signifies such petitions for things that are wanted by men, either by themselves or others; and that either for their bodies or souls, as food and raiment for the one, and discoveries of pardoning love, supplies of grace, spiritual peace, comfort, . . . for the other."

A second form of prayer is simply called "prayers." Gill commented on this second word that it signifies "good wishes and desires, directed and expressed to God for things that are in themselves to be wished for, and desired of God, either for ourselves or others." This type obviously refers to staying in constant communication with God. It involves our adoration of God and our recognition of Who He is, His holiness, Majesty, and Sovereignty.

The third form of praying mentioned here is that of intercession, which means praying on behalf of others. As Gill wrote, it "intends either complaints exhibited in prayer against others that have done injuries; or prayers put up for others, either for the averting of evil from them, or for the bestowing some good thing on them." It is when we take hold of the horns of the altar and won't let go on behalf of special needs regarding special people in our lives. It also includes interceding for revival and spiritual renewal for our community and nation.

The fourth form of prayer is that of giving thanks, "with which requests should always be made known to God," Gill wrote. Simply praising and worshipping God are the main focus of this type of praying. We come into His presence with praise and thanksgiving. We exalt Him above all the earth and acknowledge Him as the only true God. This involves a special kind of fellowship with the Heavenly Father. This is where we seek His face rather than His hand. Our purpose is to know Him better and to fellowship with Him, not have our hands out asking for what He can do for us.

It is out of our prayer life and our fasting (the denial and crucifixion of the flesh) that we have power with God to heal the sick and to cast out demons.

To Be a Minister Who Has Passion for All People

Matthew 9:11-12: "And when the Pharisees saw it, they said to His disciples, 'Why does your Teacher eat with tax collectors and sinners?' When Jesus heard that,

He said to them, 'Those who are well have no need of a physician, but those who are sick.'"

Sin-sick people are all around us, hurting people who need an answer. The people of God have the answer. The reason some churches are dying is that they are not seeking the sick and hurting.

Romans 9:2-3: ". . . that I have great sorrow and continual grief in my heart. For I could wish that I myself were accursed from Christ for my brethren, my countrymen according to the flesh."

I confess to you that I have not yet reached the place that Paul reached that he was willing to be cut off from Christ for his people, the Jews. Yet, I do have a burden. I am a desperate man, desperate for the Presence and Power of the Lord Jesus. I am desperate to see His Glory. I am desperate for revival.

I'm reminded of a young mother whose son was a member of a gang in high school. He was in trouble continually. The mother notified the authorities and the gang threatened her life and beat up her other son. Finally, she pulled her troubled son out of public school and placed him in private school. She told him that she was not going to let go of him. If he went to hell, it would be with her arms wrapped around him. Here was a desperate mother who would not give up her son to the devil. The young man finally gave his heart to God and is doing missionary work. We need more parents who will place their arms around their children and never let go.

Jude 22-23 said we would have to reach into the very fires of hell to save souls, "pulling them out of the fire, hating even the garment defiled by the flesh." Jesus said to Jerusalem, with His heart breaking, "How often I wanted to gather your children together, as a hen gathers her chicks under her wings, but you were not willing" (Matthew 23:37).

We need pastors who will place their arms around a congregation and not give up nor let go, nor let one slide into hell. There are people in hell today because of the attitudes and actions of preachers. Some seem to feel they are called to hurt, to crush, to break, to wound, to maim, or to destroy people. But I have a different calling. I am not a pallbearer, nor an undertaker, nor an executioner; I am a rescue worker. I am called to save people. I am called to heal people. I am called to encourage, to strengthen, to feed, to undergird, to comfort, and to help.

To Be a Visionary and Dreamer

Proverbs 29:18: "Where there is no vision the people perish" (King James Version [KJV]).

One of the most important elements in any minister's life is his or her vision. What motivates, preoccupies, and drives the minister? Is he or she looking forward or backward, excited about the future or living in the past?

How large is the minister's vision? Does he or she seek a task that only requires minimum effort or does it require great effort? Does he or she want to climb mountains or merely to walk up molehills? The most telling gauge of any person, but especially of a minister, is the size and configuration of that minister's vision.

Barzillai had a vision. 2 Samuel 19 shares a great story of how Barzillai provided supplies to King David, his families, and his entourage during David's exile from Jerusalem while Absalom led an insurrection. After Absalom's death, David returned to Jerusalem. Out of gratitude, he invited Barzillai to return with him. Such a dream for any man: to live in the palace, to eat the king's meat at the king's table, to enjoy the musical entertainment provided and all of the amenities of the palace.

Imagine David's surprise when Barzillai turned down his offer, saying that he, at age 80, was too old to enjoy living in the palace. He could no longer discern good from evil, nor would his taste buds tell him what he was eating, nor could he hear the music and singing. Besides all of that, he would soon die and he wanted to be buried by the graves of his father and mother.

Barzillai had a vision, but it was of a cemetery, of a grave plot, of death. He had given up on life and was simply waiting to die and be buried.

There are ministers who have compromised so many times until the lines of demarcation between right and wrong have been obliterated. They no longer have principles, standards, or integrity. They are only concerned with what is politically correct or expedient. They have lost their joy and cannot enjoy singing and dancing before the Lord. They have lost their praise and their worship. Spiritually, they are tone deaf.

What a contrast to Joshua 14 where Caleb, who was five years older than Barzillai, flexed his muscles and said that he was as strong at age 85 as he was at age 40! When the division of the land was made and Joshua asked Caleb what parcel he wanted, Caleb pointed to the mountain and said, "Give me that mountain." He then said that he would drive out the giants that inhabited the mountain.

Caleb wasn't looking for retirement or semi-retirement or some easy task. He had a vision of a battle.

His vision was driving out the giants. His vision was conquering a mountain.

How big is your vision? How tall is your mountain? What size is your enemy?

Joseph had a different configuration to his vision. He dreamed dreams. His vision was of a destiny, but it made his brothers jealous. They hated him because of his vision. Genesis 37:18-20: "And when they saw him afar off, even before he came near them, they conspired against him to kill him. Then they said one to another, 'Look, this dreamer is coming. Come therefore, and let us now kill him, and cast him into some pit, and we shall say, "Some wild beast has devoured him." We shall see what will become of his dreams!'"

His brothers threw Joseph into a pit as they contemplated his fate. Have you ever been in a pit? Maybe a church member you trusted betrayed you. Maybe it was a brother or sister you loved who betrayed you. Maybe a close friend was the perpetrator behind throwing you into a pit, selling you to a roving band of Ishmaelites, and then lying to your father saying you are dead.

You know the story. The Ishmaelites sold Joseph to Potiphar in Egypt; Potiphar's wife lied about him and Joseph wound up in prison. In prison, he met the former chief butler of Pharaoh.

Now look at the rest of the story. God wanted to get Joseph to Egypt, so he used the hatred and jealousy of his brothers to sell him to a band traveling to Egypt. Then God wanted to get Joseph an audience with the Pharaoh, so He arranged for Joseph to be sent to prison in order to meet the former butler. This man was the key in arranging an audience between Joseph and Pharaoh.

Two points stand out here. First, you might be in a pit or in a situation worse than prison. You think that God has forgotten you and your vision is dead. Remember this: God used both the pit and the prison to get Joseph to where he could see his vision come to pass.

Second, who would have thought that a butler who was a felon held the key to Joseph meeting Pharaoh? Sometimes the most seemingly inconsequential person might turn out to be the most important person to you realizing your vision.

Just because you are in a pit does not mean you are not on track to fulfill your vision and God's destiny for you. Just because you are in a type of prison does not mean you are not in the right place at the right time, that you are not right on course for God to bring you to the fulfillment of your vision. Just because your best friend is a defrocked butler in prison does not mean you do not have the right connections. Regardless of where you are right now, you may be right on course to climb your mountain and to reach God's will for your life.

God loves the dreamer, the visionary who walks with clarity and conviction toward the goal. Focused, his or her purpose in life is to fulfill the vision and bring that dream to pass.

A real dreamer is packed with potential and possibilities. A real dreamer is filled with today's gifts for tomorrow's world. A real dreamer has a *rhema* word that releases tomorrow's generation toward their destiny.

A real dreamer is a difference maker and becomes a threat to the devil and his kingdom of darkness. This causes the devil to concentrate his forces against those with a vision, those with a dream. He not only wants to kill the dream, but also the dreamer. The Bible states that the enemy comes to steal and to kill. Those who would dare to dream incur the wrath of Satan himself.

But the minister must be a dreamer, must have a vision. Regardless of the perils and the dangers, God still plants dreams and visions in the mind and spirit of the minister. God still calls ministers who will neither look to the right nor the left, who understand that He is a "right now" God for a "right now" world. God is calling for somebody who will look beyond what the forecasters call a dark and dismal future, and see the brightness and glory of unlimited possibilities. God needs someone who will confess that regardless of how dangerous or perilous the journey might be, he or she will carry the dream until God brings it to pass.

I may weep through some midnights, but I will be true to God's vision in my life. I may walk through some storms, but I must not lose sight of the dream God sowed in my spirit. I may walk alone at times, but I must be true to the calling of God. Regardless of the hounds of hell, sunny days or dark days, whether I am feeling strong or weak, I can never abandon the call, the dream, the vision God has entrusted to me.

Through the storm, through the battle, through the pain, God will see you through just as He did for Joseph. There came a day when Joseph stood before Pharaoh as the second in command of all Egypt.

Dare to dream big dreams.

Dream of hope where there is hopelessness.

Dream of great days and brighter tomorrows.

Dream of healings and miracles and deliverance.

Dream of revival and renewal.

Dream of the coming of the Lord and of heaven.
Dream of mentoring adults and empowering youth.
Dream of drug-free teens and college graduates.
Dream of cures for AIDS and cancer and diabetes.
Dream of unity in the Body of Christ.

Habakkuk 2:3: "For the vision is yet for an appointed time; But at the end it will speak, and it will not lie. Though it tarries, wait for it; Because it will surely come, it will not tarry."

To Be Ethical

The reason I have placed this section on ethics in the chapter on what God has called ministers to be rather than the chapter on what God has called ministers to do is because what we *do* comes out of what we *are*. That is, *being* precedes *doing*.

Being a minister is not conforming yourself to a code of conduct, but is, instead, being conformed to God. As God's children, we are in relationship to Him by which we are changed from being estranged sinners into the very children of God. "The Spirit Himself bears witness with our spirit that we are children of God, And if children, then heirs – heirs of God and joint heirs with Christ, if indeed we suffer with Him, that we may also be glorified together" (Romans 8:16-17). Through our relationship with God, through salvation, sanctification, and the Baptism of the Holy Spirit, through our interaction with God's Word, God is preparing us to be the people – and the ministers – who represent Him as His children.

As God's children, we will behave as God's children. "As obedient children, not conforming yourselves to the former lusts, as in your ignorance; But as He who called you is holy, you also be holy in all your conduct, Because it is written, 'Be holy, for I am holy'" (1 Peter 1:14-16). Being the children of God means that we act in ways consistent with God and God's character: that is, as our Father is holy, so are we to be holy. Our actions reflect God's holiness.

Here is a simple definition of this behavior: Ministers should conduct themselves in a way that reflects the holiness of God, our status as the children of God, and the holiness God has imparted to us; and this conduct should be toward everyone: God, family, church, business, public, sinners, poor. Jesus Himself established the criteria for those relationships when He stated we should love the Lord our God with all of our mind, soul, and strength, and love our neighbor as ourselves. He combined the entire Ten Commandments into only two: love God one hundred percent; love everyone else as you love yourself. If we love God – and He is first in our lives – then our priorities are in order and everything else will fall into place. If we love other people as we do ourselves, then we will never mistreat or hurt them.

I have been bothered by what I believe to be a lack of "love God, love neighbor" morality among ministers. Sadly, the ministry today is often demeaned by Christians and non-Christians alike precisely because of moral failure. Here are a few suggestions for behavior (again, these must be predicated upon *who you are* in God).

First, the minister should do a day's work for a day's pay. To receive the rewards and benefits of labor never rendered represents God and the church badly. Ministers must be conscientious regarding our responsibilities.

Second, respect other ministers, whether those over you in the Lord or those in your charge. Provide your senior pastor with the advice and wisdom you have gained through your study and experience. Give to your staff members a positive environment in which to labor for God. Do not take advantage of a situation in a church (for example, by using your influence to break people away from the church). Do not hinder the influence of another minister (such as a pastor's successor or predecessor). Do not build up yourself by tearing down someone else. In short, respect other ministers as you wish to be respected.

Third, do not break confidentiality. When someone has come to you privately, honor that trust. Do not share information with people who are not supposed to be privy to the information.

Fourth, be a minister of your word as well as of the Word. When you tell someone you will do something, do it. When you pledge yourself to an office, then do the very best you can. When you enter into an agreement, honor it.

Fifth, be loyal to God, to the Church, to other ministers, to friends, to family, and to your responsibilities. Never betray those who trust you.

Sixth, take a stand whether it is popular or not if you believe it is right. Do not test the wind: test only the rightness of your conviction.

Seventh, be humble in all your relationships. Pride has turned many great men and women of God, many who had a passion to serve God and God alone, into self-seekers. Understand that you are a servant; you are not the Master.

Eighth, protect your reputation. Paul did not partake of everything he believed was available to him simply because he refused to be a stumbling-block to sinners. Do not let your reputation suffer to where you are no longer able to minister to the lost and to your flock.

Ninth, treat others with love. Rather than using the Bible as a club, use the Spirit of God dwelling in you to reach out to a lost and dying world, to embrace fellow Christians and ministers with the swaddling clothes of God's infinite love.

As God's children, we have been changed. As God's ministers, we have specific duties. The minister's life – every word, every deed, every attitude – speaks the truth of our relationship with God.

To Be a Spiritual Leader

The minister is a leader. Whether it is leading a soul to salvation as an evangelist or leading a congregation as shepherd or leading a denomination as Bishop, the minister is a leader. What sets the minister apart from secular leaders is the Spirit-filled experience.

The world and the Church need Spirit-filled leaders, both men and women. These will heal the hurts of society, will lead the work of bringing in the Kingdom of God, and will see that His will is done on earth as it is in heaven (Matthew 6:10).

To be a Spirit-filled leader, the kind that makes a difference, one must be at peace with God and comfortable with oneself. The Spirit-filled leader must learn to live in his or her own "mansion."

The mansion concept is presented by Reed Bradford in a book titled *A Teacher's Quest* (Provo, Utah. Brigham Young University Press, 1971). He suggests that an individual can develop an internal "mansion" that will give dignity and joy each day, regardless of circumstances or experience. However, only Jesus can build within a person this internal mansion. Only He can give one the ability to have personal fulfillment with dignity and joy in spite of circumstances. God gives Spirit-filled leaders confidence and contentment.

Spirit-filled leadership enables men and women to match the times. Events and circumstances converge when people prepare themselves to be used of God. The Holy Spirit always prepares the person for the situation. There is a power and anointing that intensifies and magnifies whatever natural gifts, abilities, and plans the Spirit-filled leader will use. When a people, an organization, or a movement has accomplished outstanding tasks or achieved dazzling feats, they followed, as a rule, leaders who were not afraid to lead.

The purpose of Spirit-filled leadership is to benefit the followers, not to enrich the leaders. Spirit-filled leaders manage things and lead people, instead of leading things and managing people. They inspire and motivate; they do not intimidate and manipulate. Spirit-filled leaders take more than their share of the blame when things go wrong, and less than their share of credit when plans succeed.

God calls you to be a minister. This means that you will be a compassionate and forgiving servant, a prepared watchman who treats all people ethically, and a miracle-expecting, anointed, spiritual leader and visionary with a passion for people.

God calls you to be a leader. In other words, He calls you to be a difference maker.

Chapter 5

What Has God Called You to Do?

Isaiah 61:1: "The Spirit of the Lord is upon me, because the Lord has anointed Me to preach good tidings to the poor; He has sent Me to heal the broken-hearted, to proclaim liberty to the captives, and the opening of the prison to those who are bound; to proclaim the acceptable year of the Lord, and the day of vengeance of our God; to comfort all who mourn, to console those who mourn in Zion, to give them beauty for ashes, the oil of joy for mourning; the garment of praise for the spirit of heaviness; that they may be called trees of righteousness, the planting of the Lord that He may be glorified."

To Preach the Word

Preach, preach, preach, preach, preach. God has chosen through the foolishness of preaching to save the world.

You are to preach the Word, not the philosophies of man. You are not an entertainer or performer. You are a preacher. A preacher of the Word. Use stories, testimonies, illustrations, and humor to clarify or emphasize the Word, but never allow these helps to become the main message.

The devil hates the Word. The world hates the Word. The Bible is ridiculed from every area and segment of society. In Alabama, Judge Moore was removed from office because of the Word (the Ten Commandments). San Antonio pastor and author John Hagee's sermon series on Islam in America – comparing the beliefs of Muslims and Christians – was dropped from a Canadian television station in 2003 because the tone of his voice was considered by the Toronto station CTS Program Manager to be an incitement of hatred.

The Canadian House of Commons passed a bill in 2003 specifying sexual orientation as a protected class of people. Some analysts say that religious writings including the Jewish Torah, the Christian Bible, and the Muslim Quran could be classified as "hate literature" for their condemnation of homosexual behavior.

Joshua Davey, a student at a Christian college in Kirkland, Washington, was stripped of his state scholarship after he declared a double major in pastoral ministries and business/management administration (Locke v. Davey, 2003). The state's position was based upon a state law which prohibits scholarships for students who major in theology. Yet students can receive scholarship money to major in comparative religions.

Who would have believed that such restrictions would ever be enforced against religious freedom in

America? In Canada? How can a person be taken off the air because of the *tone* of his voice? How can a well-earned scholarship be taken away because the recipient chooses to study theology?

There is indeed hatred toward the Word of God. Paul said in Romans 1:16, "For I am not ashamed of the gospel of Christ; for it is the power of God to salvation for everyone who believes; for the Jew first and also for the Greek."

John 15:3: "You are already clean because of the Word which I have spoken to you."

1 Peter 1:23: "Having been born again, not of corruptible seed but of incorruptible, through the Word of God which lives and abides forever."

Psalms 107:20: "He sent His Word, and healed them, and delivered them from their destructions."

Matthew 8:16: "When evening had come, they brought to Him many who were demon-possessed. And He cast out the spirits with a Word, and healed all who were sick."

Hebrews 1:3 speaks of the Word of Power.

Romans 10:8 speaks of the Word of Faith.

1 Corinthians 12:8 speaks of the Word of Wisdom and Knowledge.

2 Corinthians 5:19 speaks of the Word of Reconciliation.

2 Corinthians 6:7 speaks of the Word of Truth.

The devil hates the Gospel. He doesn't care if we entertain or perform, as long as the Gospel that delivers people from hell, brings hope, and gives birth to faith in the hearts of believers isn't preached.

The Gospel is the message of Jesus Christ. Today, when you go to your pharmacy, you are asked if you want the generic brand. Many times the generic is as effective as the name brand, but this is not always the case. However, I want to state unequivocally that the generic brand of religion will not do. There is no other name under heaven given among men whereby we must be saved. Jesus said the world would hate us because they hated Him. They still hate Him. It is all about Him. Preach any generic brand and you will not be bothered, but when you preach Him, when you preach Jesus Christ, the entire world gets in an uproar.

To Shake the World

You must know who you are. You must know Who called you. You must know Who your Source is and to Whom you are accountable.

You are a Preacher. A man of God. A woman of God. There isn't anybody or anything that can take your place. You are irreplaceable.

Charles R. Brown, former Dean of Divinity School, Yale University, reviewed the history of the Church and highlighted its great achievements in architecture, liturgy, art, and music. But he concluded that whenever ". . . there was lacking in all this the living voice of a living man speaking the name and under the power of the living God, there came a steady irresistible decline in the religious life of that land."

You must never underestimate the crucial significance of your preaching, nor what God has accomplished by the preached Word throughout history.

It was Jonah's reluctant preaching to the city of Ninevah that resulted in the entire city of 120,000 repenting in sackcloth and ashes.

It was Ezekiel's visionary preaching to a valley of dry bones whereby God resurrected the entire valley.

It was Jeremiah's tearful preaching that impacted a whole nation.

It was John the Baptist's preaching on repentance that caused the multitudes to hear him declare, "Behold! The Lamb of God who takes away the sin of the world" (John 1:29).

It was Simon Peter's preaching on the day of Pentecost that caused 3,000 souls to be saved.

It was Stephen's preaching that caused the council to be "cut to the heart, and they gnashed at him with their teeth" (Acts 7:54).

It was Phillip's preaching that brought revival to Samaria and great joy to that city.

It was Simon Peter's preaching to Cornelius' house that caused the Holy Spirit to fall on the Gentiles and changed the course of the Church forever.

It was the Apostle Paul's preaching before King Agrippa that caused the king to cry out to Paul, "You almost persuade me to be a Christian" (Acts 26:28).

It was Charles Finney's preaching in one city whereby it was said, "When Finney arrived there were no Christians; when he left there were no sinners."

There are sermons that, after many years, yet stand out in my own mind. James A. Cross preaching "Who knows but what God has raised you up for such a time as this." C. R. Spain's powerful sermon on "God's Little People." Dr. Charles W. Conn's masterpiece, "The Lost Coin." E.V. Cobb preaching "When God Appears, What Shall I Answer Him?" Wade H. Horton's sermon, "Hear Me One More Time," a sermon he preached in a Texas campmeeting when I was just a young preacher. His message drove me to my knees where I wept and prayed through the lunch hour and into the afternoon.

God has indeed chosen through the foolishness of preaching to save the lost.

To Preach for a Decision

The purpose of the message is to bring the congregation to a place of decision-making. The message should challenge the sinner to make a choice regarding salvation. The message should inspire the sick to believe on His Word and to receive their healing. Those who are bound by the addictions of drugs, alcohol, or pornography should be inspired to look to the Cross, believe, and receive deliverance.

The preached Word should inspire and challenge the hearers to take some type of action that brings them closer in their relationship and walk with God. They should leave the service different from what they were when they came, either saved, healed, delivered, encouraged, strengthened, comforted, committed to service, or blessed in some manner in which they will be better and stronger Christians.

To Expect Miracles

The minister must expect miracles in his or her life and ministry. According to Webster's dictionary, a miracle is "an extraordinary event manifesting divine intervention in human affairs."

God has always manifested Himself in the affairs of man. Mark 16:17 clearly says that "these signs will follow those who believe. . . ."

You don't have to have "walking on the water, mountain moving faith" for miracles to take place. Miracles take place in our lives because we are of the household of faith.

The greatest faith you can possess is that the Son of God came to this earth wrapped in a robe of flesh; was born in a manger; died on a rugged cross for our sins; was buried and rose the third day and ascended to the right hand of the Father and lives forever to make intercession for us. If you believe these truths, then you have the foundational faith to believe God for any miracle.

Go to church expecting a miracle.

Preach expecting a miracle.

Pray for anybody for anything expecting a miracle.

Get up each morning expecting a miracle that day.

God provided for miracles.

God promised miracles.

God cannot lie.

God gave us the power of attorney to use the name of Jesus when we ask for a miracle. Why wouldn't we expect a miracle? Every day? Every service? Every sermon? Every prayer?

To Heal the Brokenhearted

The minister has the power to lift up or to cast down, to speak words of hope or to speak words of discouragement, to bless or to curse, to heal or to afflict. The commandment of Scripture is to heal the brokenhearted (Isaiah 61:1). Are your hands healing hands or hurting hands? Are your words uplifting or depressing? The minister must reach out and touch the brokenhearted, the hurting, and bring healing and comfort and encouragement to them.

Luke 10:33-34: "But a certain Samaritan, as he journeyed, came where he was. And when he saw him, he had compassion. So he went to him, and bandaged his wounds, pouring on oil and wine, and he set him on his own animal, brought him to an inn, and took care of him."

This is a powerful story that sets an example for the minister. The priest and the Levite passed by the wounded and dying man. Why? Maybe they were too busy doing nonessential things. Maybe they did not want to get involved.

There are hurting, wounded people all around us. The church that cares about touching the hurting will always be a growing church.

Jesus said the Samaritan "came where he was." You cannot truly make the difference you should at long distance, holding people at arm's length. We, as ministers of God, need to be in the market place where people live; we need to touch them where they are hurting.

To Give the Garments of Praise

Throughout the Bible you read the statement, "The Word of the Lord came to. . . ." There should be such a powerful word from the Lord that the down-trodden, depressed, and those wearing the garments of mourning will be lifted up to a pinnacle of praise and rejoicing; a word that causes the hearer to cast off the sackcloth and ashes and to dance before the Lord as David danced and to sing before the Lord like Paul and Silas in the jailhouse.

Too many ministers have lost their joy, their song, and their dance. The cares and burdens of this life seem to crowd out the heavenly provisions Jesus appropriated for us on Calvary. The minister is in a battle with the world, the devil, and is at times attacked by members of his or her own congregation. Sometimes the load becomes so heavy until there seems to be no reason to sing or rejoice.

However, it is for these very reasons that the man and woman of God must touch Someone who can take the clouds away and remove the shadows of doubt, who can cast off the garments of mourning. It is for these very reasons I must have Someone – in my darkest hours or in the middle of my fiercest battles – touch me and give me a joy the world cannot understand. This Someone can indeed provide me with unspeakable joy. This Someone can restore unto me everything the devil has stolen.

I need the kind of experience that will put a smile on my face, happiness in my heart, a song in my mouth, and a dance in my feet. We all need the kind of experience that takes the broken pieces of our lives and puts them back together again.

Nehemiah 8:10: ". . . for the joy of the Lord is your strength."

Psalms 40:3: "He has put a new song in my mouth—Praise to our God."

Psalms 77:6 tells us He will give us a "song in the night." Paul and Silas experienced such a song in the Philippian jailhouse.

Psalms 100:1: "Make a joyful shout to the Lord, all you lands! Serve the Lord with gladness; come before His presence with singing. . . ."

Psalms 149:1: "Praise the Lord! Sing to the Lord a new song. . . ."

Job 36:27: "For He draws up drops of water, which distill as rain from the mist." This verse is saying that the vapor must ascend before the rains come down. Therefore, we must send up praises as a vapor in order for the rains of God's blessings to come down.

I am going to praise God at all times and in all situations and circumstances. I am not going to wait until I see results, or until I feel better, or until the pain in my body disappears, or until my financial situation improves, or until I get a promotion on my job, or until I understand every experience in my life. I am going to praise Him now. I am going to thank Him for what He has already done, for what He is now doing, and for what He is going to do.

He is worthy of all praise.

I thank Him because I am alive, because I have made it through the day, because I know that regardless of anything that happens to me, He still loves me and watches over me. I know He is still on His throne and is in control of my life.

I praise Him because of His promise in Psalms 91:11: "For He shall give His angels charge over you, to keep you in all your ways."

When you are discouraged, praise Him.

When you are hurting, praise Him.

When you are sick, praise Him.

When you are attacked by your enemies, praise Him.

When things happen to you that you don't understand, praise Him.

When your world is turned upside down, praise Him.

It won't be long until the joy that comes with the knowledge that God is on His throne and is in control of your life starts stirring new and fresh in your heart.

To Establish Boundaries

All ministers should know the lines they will not cross regardless of the circumstances and situations. I know what I want to do and want to be.

I want to keep my morality like Joseph when he left his torn coat in the hands of Potiphar's wife.

I want to have respect for God's anointed like David when he found Saul asleep in a cave and refused to take his life.

I want to have the hunger for God that Paul and David had when Paul said, "That I may know Him and the power of His resurrection, and the fellowship of His sufferings being conformed to His death (Philippians 3:10). David said, "As the deer pants for the water brooks, so pants my soul for You, O God" (Psalms 42:1).

I want to have the strength to pull down strongholds as Samson did when he pulled the pillars of the temple down on the Philistines.

I want to make the right decisions as Elisha did when he said, after being asked by Elijah what he wanted, "Please let a double portion of your spirit be upon me" (2 Kings 2:9).

I want to walk with God like Enoch did, who "walked with God; and he was not, for God took him" (Genesis 5:24).

I want to maintain my integrity as Job did when he said, "I will maintain mine own ways before the Lord" (Job 13:15 KJV). He had determined that he would continue to do what he had always done prior to losing his family, health, possessions, and influence. He was declaring that nothing had happened to him that would change who he was or how he lived. He was saying, "Devil, I'm going to keep on doing what I have always done. I prayed before and I'll keep on praying. I sang before and I'll keep on singing. I praised God before and I'll keep on praising Him. I trusted Him before and I'll keep on trusting Him."

Daniel did the same thing when he learned that by continuing to pray, he would be cast into the den of lions. He could have prayed behind closed windows. God would have heard him if he had just whispered a prayer. But Daniel understood that praying behind closed windows would be a victory for his enemies. Essentially, he said, "I'm going to do what I have always done and I will not allow the devil to change my behavior." He threw open the windows and began to pray. When you are in the valley, a storm, a battle – wherever you are – throw open the windows when you pray.

I want to have the fire of God like Jeremiah did as he said, it's "a burning fire shut up in my bones" (Jeremiah 20:9).

I want to have the courage of Shadrach, Meshach, and Abednego who refused to bow even as they watched the entire population bow before the graven image made by Nebuchadnezzar.

I want to maintain my strength like Caleb, whose attitude was, "I'm as strong today as I was 45 years ago. Give me this mountain full of giants. I'm ready for a big challenge" (Joshua 14:10-11).

I want to be a difference maker. I want my life to genuinely count for Christ. I am desperate for God, desperate for revival, desperate to see His Glory, desperate to feel His Presence and Power.

God has called you to be a difference maker. Whether you are in the mountains, valleys, or islands; whether you are in the city, town, or country; no matter where you are, He wants to anoint you and use you to bring revival to your area.

Every minister should seek to be able to say with Paul that he had wholly followed after the Lord and had declared the whole counsel of God. Paul said "I am innocent from the blood of all men" (Acts 20:26).

What are you willing to do for God? Would you stop for a blind beggar by the wayside? Jesus did. The crowd tried to silence the poor man, but Jesus heard his cry and said, "Bring him to me."

Would you travel a long way out of your way to witness to a woman who was a foreigner (Samaritan), who had been married five times, and who was living with a man who was not her husband? Jesus did.

Do you care enough about souls to go into the highways and hedges and bring people to Jesus? Jesus commanded us to do so.

Do you care enough about a crippled friend to tear off the roof of a house and let him down through a hole to get him into the presence of Christ? Four men did.

Will you leave the safety of the sheepfold and the fellowship of the 99 and go out into the treacherous, dark, and dangerous night to find one lost sheep? The good Shepherd did.

Will you stop on the Jericho road for the wounded, hurting, dying robbed victim, bind up his wounds, and then pay for his lodging until he gets well? The Good Samaritan did.

Will you beat on the door of the unjust judge and never give up until your request is granted? The persistent widow did.

When your prodigal son has taken money he never earned and wasted it on harlots, but finally returned home, will you run to meet him, throw your arms around him, and kill the fatted calf so that he can have a party with his friends? His father did.

Will you build your house and your ministry upon the solid Rock and not on sinking sand? The wise man did.

To Walk Worthy

The writer of Ephesians said for us to walk worthy (4:1).

Acts 5:40-41: "And they agreed with him, and when they had called for the apostles and beaten them, they commanded that they should not speak in the name of Jesus, and let them go. So they departed from the presence of the council, rejoicing that they were counted worthy to suffer shame for His name." Did they depart discouraged? No! Depressed? No! Confused? No! Weeping? No!

No, I don't want to be beaten or thrown in prison, but I do want to be counted worthy. Whatever any of us faces in the future – and this we do not know, but we know we live in perilous, difficult times – we must pray that we will be found worthy. God holds the future, but I want to be worthy.

Earlier, I mentioned well-known preachers who are guilty of questionable practices and doctrine. This is not the only generation to endure such people.

2 Peter 2:1-3: "But there were also false prophets among the people, even as there will be false teachers among you, who will secretly bring in destructive heresies, even denying the Lord who bought them and bring on themselves swift destruction. And many will follow their destructive ways, because of whom the way of truth will be blasphemed. By covetousness they will exploit you with deceptive words; for a long time their judgment has not been idle, and their destruction does not slumber."

2 Peter 2:14: "Having eyes full of adultery and that cannot cease from sin, enticing unstable souls. They have a heart trained in covetous practices, and are accursed children."

2 Peter 2:17: "These are wells without water, clouds carried by a tempest, for whom is reserved the blackness of darkness forever."

There are many who are not worthy. There are many who put their faith in the things of this world, believing that their future is secure by their power or wealth or position or fame. They betray their calling as they betray God.

But God will have a people and a ministry. Let us walk with God, worthy.

To Deal with the Valleys

Possibly the most effective tool the devil has is the tool of discouragement. It is amazing how easily we become discouraged.

God performed all of the miracles in Egypt in order to set Israel free from their bondage. He divided the Red Sea, but the Children of Israel murmured and complained: "Because there were no graves in Egypt, have you taken us away to die in the wilderness?" (Exodus 14:11).

While they stared at the pillar of cloud and the pillar of fire, they doubted and complained.

While they ate manna from the ovens of heaven, they doubted and complained.

While they drank water from the rock, they doubted and complained.

While they wore clothes and shoes that would not wear out, they doubted and complained.

They had seen the Presence of God at the foot of the mountain. They had seen the fire on the mountain. Yet, they still doubted and complained.

Yes, discouragement is a powerful tool of Satan against the minister.

Elijah prayed fire down from heaven and had the prophets of Baal put to death. Immediately, you find him under a juniper tree asking God to kill him.

The pastor preaches a powerful sermon on Sunday morning, sees the altar filled with seekers weeping their way through to salvation, and witnesses miracle after miracle. Then, on Monday morning something goes awry and you find him sitting under a juniper tree discouraged and telling God he is quitting the ministry. Plunging from the mountaintop to the lowest valley, the descent is swift.

How can one see the manifest glory of God one minute and, in the next minute, question God and try to resign from the ministry? It happens all too often.

This is the valley syndrome. Everybody goes there at some time or other. It is a more popular destination than Disney World or Gatlinburg, more popular than the Riviera or Acapulco.

If you find yourself in the valley, understand where you are. You have a different view of things than when you were on the mountaintop. On the mountaintop, you believed you could cast out demons and tread on serpents; but in the valley your surroundings look much different. In the valley, the mountains tower over you and look down on you. You can only see your immediate surroundings. You lose perspective. In the valley, your circumstances blot out the larger picture; your depth perception doesn't work properly. You appear smaller and more insignificant. You appear as a grasshopper in your own eyes. You cannot see around the corner or over the hill. You cannot see the solution or answer to your situation until it is right there in front of you.

When you are in the valley, you can lose your vision. Your vision becomes blurred and everything seems out of focus. In the valley, you can lose your perspective.

How can you keep Sunday's victory on Monday? You must check your heart. You cannot get to the mountain with sin in your life, or with hard feelings against your brother, or with the wrong spirit and motives, or with an unforgiving attitude or bitterness toward anyone.

Then, after you have had a heart checkup, after everything is in order, start praising the Lord. Better yet, in the midst of your valley, begin to praise Him. Praise Him in good times and bad times. You cannot praise Him very long without the gloom lifting; then, you will find yourself moving toward the mountaintop.

This type of valley or mountain isn't a physical place: it's a state of mind, a state of spiritual victory or spiritual depression.

"Yea though I walk through the valley of the shadow of death, I will fear no evil; for You are with me" (Psalms 23:4).

My word to you is that you can walk through the valley and live on the mountaintop. While walking through the darkest moment and toughest time of your life, you can still enjoy a mountaintop experience. Because I've been to the mountain, I have joy unspeakable and full of glory! I have a praise on my lips and a song in my heart.

Minister, you must learn to deal with adversity, discouragement, and doubting. Refuse to stay in the valley. Only when you stand on the mountaintop can you see clearly and get a panoramic view of God's will for your life. Never make a decision regarding your future while walking in the valley.

When you are on the mountain, miracles take place in your life.

It was when Dr. King was on the mountain that he saw the glory of the coming of the Lord.

It was when Enoch was on the mountain that he walked with God and was not because God took him.

It was when Moses was on the mountain that he saw an entire mountain on fire with the presence of God.

It was when Elijah was on the mountain that he saw fire fall from heaven and burn up the sacrifice.

It was when Daniel opened his windows and looked toward Jerusalem that he saw the mountain. That night, he slept like a baby with his head pillowed on the mane of a lion.

It was when Ezekiel went to the mountain that he saw a wheel in the middle of a wheel.

But the valley does not mean defeat. *Live* on the mountain, but merely *walk through* the valley.

Job, walking through the deepest valley of his life, made it to the mountaintop and said, "I know my Redeemer liveth."

Stephen was being stoned by the Pharisees, Sadducees and hypocrites, but made it to the mountaintop in his dying moment and said, "I see Jesus standing at the right hand of the Father."

Paul and Silas sang songs at midnight in a Philippian jailhouse, even though their backs had been beaten because they had been to the mountain.

When discouragement, doubting, or complaining tries to take root in your life, recognize that the devil is trying to bog you down in the valley. Instead, begin to seek the God of the valley and of the mountain.

To Wage Spiritual Warfare

Ephesians 6:12: "For we do not wrestle against flesh and blood, but against principalities, against powers, against the rulers of the darkness of this age, against spiritual hosts of wickedness in the heavenly places."

We are at war. We must be equipped to do battle.

1 Peter 5:8: "Be sober, be vigilant; because your adversary the devil walks about as a roaring lion, seeking whom he may devour."

Notice, in this Scripture, that the intent of the devil is not to take prisoners, but to devour or destroy the believers in Christ. His strategy in this warfare is to establish as many strongholds as possible in the life of the believer, especially the minister, in order to have as many launching pads as possible from which to attack you. These strongholds might be sin or conditions that will lead to sin, such as discouragement, anger, bitterness, revenge, flirtations with sin, addictions (such as pornography), pleasure-seeking, and greed.

People who have confided in me reveal certain tactics of the devil. Often, curiosity truly does "kill the cat." Take the case of pornography. Some think, what harm will come from a slight flirtation with pornography? So, they steal a glance at it, perhaps visiting sexually oriented Web sites. But then, they find themselves addicted. Pornography is one of those deadly sins because it may appear non-threatening on its surface. A leading denomination sent a questionnaire to its ministers asking them to respond anonymously. Of those who responded, 65 percent admitted that pornography was a problem in their own lives.

Yes, the devil uses easy temptations to beguile God's ministers, tricking many into believing that they are doing nothing truly wrong, truly harmful. But then comes the downward spiral.

Another example: Feelings of anger or bitterness or the desire to seek revenge for some wrong (or perceived wrong) may seem justified, but harboring those feelings will create in you a damaged, scarred spirit. And, feeding anger and bitterness can lead to committing an injustice. Did you know that you can be right and still be wrong?

An injustice to you does not justify committing an injustice. Paul tells us that "the weapons of our warfare are not carnal but mighty in God for pulling down strongholds" (2 Corinthians 10:4). If we use carnal weapons, we can only reap the benefits of what carnal weapons can accomplish. But if we use the weapons that are mighty through God, then we can reap the benefits of the weapons God uses on our behalf.

The devil will often use an innocent friend or family member to feed your self-pity or your outrage. Through this affirmation of your bad feelings and of your warped perception of what is right and justifiable, a molehill becomes a mountain.

Ahithophel was a counselor to King David, but when David had an adulterous affair with Ahithophel's granddaughter, Bathsheba, he never forgave David. Bitter, he joined Absalom in an attempt to overthrow the king. David repented his sin (read Psalms 51, a great prayer of repentance) and God established David's throne forever. But Ahithophel, innocent in David's sin, never overcame his sense of David's betrayal. He finally committed suicide.

Again, you can be right and wind up being wrong. You can allow someone else's sin toward you to destroy you.

If you are hurt or bitter toward any individual and feel you are incapable of forgiving that person, you must first make a decision to forgive. Forgiveness isn't a feeling: it is a choice. Then the Holy Spirit will internalize within you the decision you make.

Every stronghold of Satan weakens the founda-tion of your Christian experience and hinders your fellowship and relationship with God. How do we deal with the various strategies of Satan? How do we wage spiritual warfare?

First, do your best to avoid temptation. Don't give the devil a target to shoot at. Jesus stressed the importance of avoiding temptation in the Lord's Prayer. He said, "do not lead us into temptation but deliver us from the evil one" (Matthew 6:13). Again, He commanded us to "abstain from every form of evil" (1 Thessalonians 5:22).

Very few Christians set out to do evil or wrong. They simply begin by entertaining the thought of something, believing that they can at any time brush the thought aside. They think that *they are in control.* But as the fascination grows and the power of that thought – or of what is behind it – increases its hold upon them, they realize that they have lost control. The control they actually had was to make the decision not to flirt with sin in the beginning. James 1:15: "Then when desire has conceived, it gives birth to sin; and sin, when it is full-grown, brings forth death."

What else must we do to wage spiritual warfare? Waging spiritual warfare requires vigilance against the temptations of Satan. It requires a close walk with God so that when temptations get through your own defenses, God's protections will keep you safe. It requires knowledge of the Word to counter the devil's seductive lies. It requires letting go of negative feelings, those that drain you of your spiritual vitality, so that you can move forward without baggage. It requires focusing on God's call so that you remain where God wants you to be in your life. It requires serving God and people so that you are not so self-absorbed that you are an easy target for the devil. It requires an attitude of praise, a mighty weapon at all times against Satan's temptations.

To Endure Hardship as a Good Soldier
2 Timothy 2:3: "You therefore must endure hardship as a good soldier of Jesus Christ."

Tough times come to the minister, who must never forsake his or her post of duty. The hireling flees, but the good soldier will always be at the place assigned by the Commander-in-Chief. The work of God is more than a duty: it is an honor.

The following story circulated on the Internet and was published in a number of association newsletters, but without any author identification (I have reproduced with some paraphrasing): The Third Infantry Regiment at Fort Myer has the responsibility for providing ceremonial units and honor guards for state occasions, White House social functions, public celebrations, interments at Arlington National Cemetery, and standing a very formal sentry watch at the Tombs of the Unknowns. The public is familiar with the precision of what is called "walking post" at the Tombs. From roped-off galleries, visitors can form to observe the troopers, their measured step, and their almost mechanical silent rifle shoulder changes. They are relieved every hour in a very formal drill. Some people believe that when the Cemetery is closed to the public, this show stops. But to the men who are dedicated to this work, it is no show: it is a "charge of honor." The formality and precision continue uninterrupted all night. During the nighttime, the drill of relief and the measured step of the on-duty sentry remain unchanged from the daylight hours. To these men – these special men – the continuity of this post is the key to the honor and respect shown to the honored dead, symbolic of all Americans unaccounted for, the American combat dead.

The story continues: During hurricane Isabel, with thousands of trees down, power outages, traffic signals out, roads filled with downed limbs and debris, and flooding, the Regimental Commander of the U.S. Third Infantry sent word to the nighttime Sentry Detail to secure the post and to seek shelter from the high winds. This command was given to ensure personal safety of this guard. But they disobeyed the order. During winds that turned over vehicles and turned debris into projectiles, the measured step continued.

According to this story, the soldiers who refused to seek personal safety did so because guarding the Tomb was not just an assignment: it was the highest honor that could be afforded to a service person. The tomb has been patrolled continuously, 24 hours per week, seven days per week, since 1930.

My point is this: God has called us to service. We are to be faithful regardless of the danger. It is more than a duty. It is more than an assignment. *It is an honor.*

Yes, in the ministry there are battles, persecutions, hardships, and misunderstandings. But we have our assignments. Like those "walking the posts" at the tombs, we must stand our guard regardless of how strong the winds or how fierce the storm. We are on watch with souls at stake. Our assignment is more than a duty: it is an honor.

To Nurture the Family

There seem to be many misunderstandings regarding the relationship and responsibilities of the minister and his or her family. Every believer – especially the minister – must understand that God comes first and everything else follows. We are to seek first the Kingdom of God and His righteousness (Matthew 6:33). We must never allow anyone or anything to separate us from God, nor to hinder our relationship with the Lord.

There are ministers, though, who are so married to the Church that they forget the priority the Lord places upon the family.

The family is the first institution God ever created on this earth. "Therefore a man shall leave his father and mother and be joined to his wife, and they shall become one flesh" (Genesis 2:24).

God used the family as the pattern for His relationship with Israel. He declared in Isaiah 54:5, "For your Maker is your Husband, The Lord of hosts is His name; And your Redeemer is the Holy One of Israel; He is called the God of the whole earth." Paul said in Ephesians 3:15, "from whom the whole family in heaven and earth is named." And in Hosea 2:2, God spoke of Israel's spiritual sins and stated, "She is not my wife and I am not her husband."

2 Corinthians 11:2: "For I am jealous for you with godly jealousy. For I have betrothed you to one husband, that I may present you as a chaste virgin to Christ."

Revelation 19:7: "Let us be glad and rejoice and give Him glory, for the marriage of the Lamb has come, and His wife has made herself ready."

Ephesians 5:25, 28-29: "Husbands, love your wives, just as Christ also loved the Church and gave Himself for her. . . . So husbands ought to love their own wives as their own bodies; he who loves his wife loves himself. For no one ever hated his own flesh, but nourishes and cherishes it, just as the Lord does the church." This more graphically illustrates the "one flesh" of husband and wife.

1 Corinthians 7:3: "Let the husband render to his wife the affection due her, and likewise also the wife to the husband."

When we understand the emphasis God places upon the family and the relationship between husband

and wife, we can understand God's view of His relationship with Israel and the relationship between Christ and the Church. The church is the family amplified. The family is the church in microcosm. God expects the minister to be as affectionate, as caring, as loving, as providing, and as protecting toward his or her family as God is to the Body of Christ. The minister can only do this as he or she models the right relationship with God. The husband who merely provides for the natural and physical needs of his family and neglects their spiritual needs, is not a true provider for his family. The wife and mother who works diligently in the church but ignores her family is not a true nurturer.

Nothing is more beautiful than a godly husband and wife living out God's plan and purpose for their lives. This is a true spiritual union. Just as we nurture our relationship with God through attention, communication (prayer), and understanding (the Word), we must nurture this relationship through constant vigilance.

When children come into this relationship, it adds a level of responsibility that has existed since Adam and Eve became parents. Even as the minister has a responsibility to God, so he or she has a responsibility to offspring. God does not expect His men and women to abandon their duties to their families. Of course, all human relationships are prioritized below our responsibility to God. Too many ministers have focused so much on their ministries that they have forgotten those whom God has specifically entrusted to them: their families.

Jesus stated that the person (minister) who does not provide for his own family was worse than an infidel. What does the word "provide" entail? I believe it includes spiritual, mental, emotional, psychological, physical, and financial provision.

The minister should see that all of the family's needs are met. To do this means to provide quality time with them; to train them in the ways of the Lord Jesus Christ; to model true biblical Christianity; to mentor them and nurture them so that they, too, will grow up loving the Lord in such a manner that God will delight and receive joy from their lives.

Within the context of the love we have for God, we also love our families. We *extend* and *represent* the love of God *to* our wives, husbands, children, and parents. We model the love of God and the dedication of God to us to those given to us by God.

Chapter 6

The Rewards of the Minister

No job or position in the world offers rewards equal to the rewards of the ministry. What can be greater than seeing some drunk stagger into your service and, after hearing you preach, stagger to an altar, pray, and get up cold sober rejoicing in his newfound experience?

What can be greater than seeing a home that is broken and heading toward divorce, leaving children devastated, restored? What can be greater than seeing the formerly estranged couple standing hand in hand at the altar after hearing you preach?

What can be greater than seeing wayward boys and girls who are strung out on drugs weep their way to a saving knowledge of Jesus Christ? What can be greater than hearing them testify about their deliverance from such addictions?

What can be greater than seeing the oppressed and depressed find the joy of the Lord that lights up their faces after they have heard and received the Word of Power in their hearts?

What can be greater than having some be-reaved, tragedy-stricken person grab your hand after a sermon and say, "Your message has given me hope and comfort. I don't think I could have made it without the Word today"?

What can be greater than witnessing the shiftless and irresponsible be touched by the Holy Spirit, find a job, then become model citizens of the community?

What can be greater than seeing a broken-hearted mother, who has prayed for her husband or son or daughter for years, rejoice through her tears as she witnesses her loved ones receive Christ?

What can be greater than being the instrument God uses to bring revival to a city or nation?

What can be greater than using God's Word to shine the light of Truth in dark places?

What can be greater than tearing down Satan's strongholds by the power of God's Holy Spirit?

What can be greater than impacting society by sharing with the world the love and example of Jesus Christ?

Yes, even though you may have suffered hardship, adversity, sacrifice, and persecution, the rewards far outweigh any difficulties. Why? Because you are called of God. You are a difference maker. Whether it is to awaken a sleeping church or a sleeping nation, or to witness to one dying soul, you are called to make a difference.

You may be reading this and thinking that the devil has been tempting you to quit the ministry. May I say to you that You Can't Quit.

You can't quit!

Eleazer gripped the handle of the sword so hard fighting the Philistines until, when the battle was over, he could not turn loose of the sword. His flesh was embedded in the handle of the sword, and the sword was embedded in the flesh of his hand. He gripped the sword until finally the sword gripped him.

That is the way it is with the ministry. Many leave the ministry every year. May I say this kindly and with great compassion? I don't believe a God-called man or woman can simply walk away from the ministry. There is a time when you grip your calling, but then your calling grips you. You can't turn it loose.

Jesus asked the burning question to His disciples as the multitude turned away because of His hard sayings: "Do you also want to go away?" They replied simply, "Lord, to whom shall we go? You have the words of eternal life" (John 6:67-68).

Let me tell you two stories, each one of God's calling, each one of decision. The first is about a successful minister of many years ago. Before his call, he had married a woman from a wealthy family. After his call, and after establishing himself in the ministry, his wife divorced him, claiming she would not be married to a minister. The man's supervisor told him that he could not minister as a divorced man, so he redirected his life, becoming a very successful businessman.

A few months before his death, this man shared with me his deep feelings of failure. He felt God's call on his life but, in tears, he was haunted by the decision he had made not to be God's minister.

The second story is of Martha Jane Woodard, the mother-in-law of Dr. T. L. Lowery. At age 90, she retired as a pastor. Prior to her death at age 91, she lamented her decision to stop preaching. Her daughter, Mildred, asked, "Where will you preach, mother, since you have given up your church?" This precious lady, with the fire of God's call still burning in her inner-most being, replied "On the street corner. There are street corners all over Columbus, Georgia."

Two callings. Two paths. At the end of each life, there was still the call. For one, there was sadness, a sense of failure. For the other, there was determination, a drive to still respond, "Yes, Lord, I am Your minister!"

My question to you is this? If you were to leave the ministry, where would you go? The calling has gripped you and won't turn you loose.

If I were to quit preaching, where would I go and what would I do?

Drive a taxicab?

Sell cars or real estate?

Play golf every day?

Fish or hunt?

Make life miserable for my wife and have her divorce me?

I *can't*. The calling has me and I can't get loose.

When every soul is saved, and every believer is healed, and every discouraged person is encouraged and strengthened, and every bereaved person is comforted, then maybe I can slow down; but now I can't.

I am a preacher.

You can't quit, either. Because of health or other reasons, you may have to redirect your ministry by retiring from pastoring or from some other type of ministry, but you won't retire from the ministry. You don't quit preaching. Why?

You are a preacher.

You are a difference maker.

Chapter 7

Conclusion

A friend of mine shared this true story with me. Before fire departments were mechanized, his grandfather worked for the fire department in Mobile, Alabama. The fire engines were pulled by horses, and the fire chief's buggy was pulled by a beautiful horse named Dan.

When the fire departments became mechanized, they looked for places where the horses could be retired and taken care of. My friend's grandfather asked for Dan, stating they had a nice green pasture with a good barn and plenty of water. The department gave Dan to him and soon Dan was enjoying the life of luxury, a life of retirement with plenty of room, shelter, food, and water.

There was only one problem. Every time Dan heard the fire engine's siren, he would jump the fence and go to the fire. They couldn't build a fence high enough to keep Dan whenever he heard the alarm.

The family knew when the alarm sounded that it was a waste of time to go to the pasture. Instead, they would immediately go to the fire and, sure enough, there Dan would be, standing quietly by. He didn't get in the way, nor did he disturb anything. He was doing what he had been trained to do: go to the fire at the sound of the alarm.

Like Dan, the minister has been trained to go to the fire and to rescue souls sliding into hell's fire. Every time the alarm sounds, the God-called man and woman does one thing: go to the fire. That is what they have been called to do. That is what they have been trained to do.

You, dear minister, have the greatest calling in the universe. You are a preacher. God has called you to make a difference. By His calling, by His anointing, by His grace, by His power, by His Spirit, you are a difference maker!

About the Author

Dr. Robert White responded to God's call on his life to be a minister of the Gospel more than 40 years ago. Since that time, he has traveled to more than 100 countries and conducted crusades, seminars, and conferences in nearly 60 countries.

Dr. White has served his denomination as pastor, evangelist, seminary president, and world missions director. In 1994, his peers elected him to his denomination's highest executive position. In addition, he has served on the Board of Administration and Nominating Committee of the National Association of Evangelicals.

Currently an international evangelist, Dr. White received his D.Min. from Trinity Lutheran Seminary. He also holds a B.A. from Rocky Mountain College and an M.A. from Arizona State University.